Angel

Melodies

A LITTLE GUIDE TO WINNING AT LIFE & LOVE AT ANY STAGE OF THE GAME!

As a writing coach and trainer to hundreds of authors at Author Academy Elite, I am thrilled about Francesca Bellamore's book. Her guide is a game-changer and will serve as a great asset to people who want to win in life and love, especially parents that aim to raise happy and healthy children.

—Kary Oberbrunner, Founder of Author Academy Elite, author of *ELIXIR PROJECT, Day Job to Dream Job, The Deeper Path and Your Secret Name.*

In a culture where ***winning*** often becomes an all-consuming obsession, Francesca Bellamore reminds us about what ***really*** matters most. When love is the foundation of our lives, even imperfect humans can choose to play the role of first-class angels. The stories in this book will inspire gratitude and encourage growth toward a more meaningful life.

—Teri Capshaw, Author of *Dying to Win: How to Inspire and Ignite Your Child's Love of Learning in an Overstressed World*

Francesca Bellamore has written a beautiful book that spoke to my heart, and I am certain that it will speak to yours as well. *Angel Melodies: A Little Guide to Winning at Life and Love at any Stage of the Game*, is a very powerful book. The stories Francesca shares will tug at your heartstrings. I realized through reading the pages of this book, and the beautiful stories throughout, that I am surrounded by more first-class angels than I ever realized. Even more impactful, I discovered the importance of me being a first-class angel to others. Music lovers will especially be gripped by the intertwining of stories and melodies. I will honestly read this book again!

—Kelly Renee' Baker – author of *Defeating Your Greatest Opponent: Seven Decisions You Must Make to Become a Champion in Life*

Read, reflect and apply the wisdom in *Angel Melodies: A Little Guide to Winning at Life & Love at any Stage of the Game,* you will strengthen your prayer life; you will grow in your walk with God; you will deepen your relations with others by a sacred connection with them and God as you read this book. I recommend it enthusiastically to you.

—Pat Gano – John Maxwell Coach, Trainer, Speaker, and Author of *The Language of Heaven: 5 Gifts that Create Legacy*

Angel Melodies

Angel Melodies

A LITTLE GUIDE TO WINNING AT LIFE & LOVE AT ANY STAGE OF THE GAME!

FRANCESCA BELLAMORE

ANGEL MELODIES
A LITTLE GUIDE TO WINNING AT LIFE & LOVE AT ANY STAGE OF THE GAME

Printed in the United States of America
Published by Author Academy Elite
PO Box 43, Powell, OH 43035
www.AuthorAcademyElite.com

Cover design by 99designs.com

Scripture reference excerpts are from Saint Benedict Press New American Bible, TAN Books, Charlotte, NC (www.tanbooks.com) and have been used with permission.

Paperback: 978-1-64085-161-0
Hardback: 978-1-64085-162-7
Ebook: 978-1-64085-163-4
Library of Congress: 2017916155

This book contains many stories about life and love. The names of several people have been changed to protect the privacy of individuals whose lives served as an inspiration for the stories contained in this book. Facts, conversations, identities, and circumstances might have been changed or eliminated to further protect the privacy of persons or institutions. Other facts have been changed or rearranged to teach valuable lessons about life and love. Therefore, this book should be regarded as realistic fiction.

The information contained in this book is not intended to override the common sense, wisdom, or knowledge of any person. Nor is meant to serve as a substitution for nutritional, psychological or medical expertise. Readers seeking nutritional, psychological, or medical advice or assistance should consult a competent and licensed professional.

Dedication

This book is dedicated to my children who are first-class angels still in training.

This book is also dedicated to all the first-class angels in my life and the lives of my children.

Table of Contents

Dedication vii

1   Prelude to Angel Melodies. 1

2   Wrestling with Life & Death. 16

3   Momma Bird Flies from the Nest 20

4   First-Class Angels in Training 35

5   The Welcoming Angels 40

6   How to Mend a Rift 47

7   Little Things that Make Life
    Easier & Breezier 63

8   God Sent a Fleet of First-Class Angels 82

9   Tales of a Comfort Food Queen 95

10   The Tempest. 100

11   Advanced Halo Hints 108

12   The Aftermath of the Storm 120

13   A Long Road to Recovery 126

14 Our Earth Angels 141

15 Sunshine Therapy 147

16 Lifting Minds & Heart Through
   Music & the Arts 154

17 Meddling with Love 160

18 Baby Bird Flies from the Nest 164

19 How to Befriend First-Class Angels 170

20 To Wear a Helmet or Not Wear a Helmet? 177

21 The Helmet-Maker 187

22 Crossed Signals 190

23 For the Love of the Athlete 196

24 Wow, Just Wow! 205

25 Heads Up 215

26 Bless Your Heart 225

27 Fall into the Pool of Love 229

28 Tennis Anyone? 237

29 Exercising the Heart Muscle 240

30 Amen! 245

31 When the Dream Ends 250

32 A Great Lover & Fighter 257

33 Glory to Glory 267

34 Building Up Our Spiritual Muscles 275

35 "Love It Up" 277

36 Final String of Halo Hints 282

   Endnotes 285

   Counting My Blessings 289

   About the Author 301

CHAPTER 1

Prelude to Angel Melodies

In the beginning, my writing was meant to be a collection of memories of one of my amazing friends who died of cancer when we were thirty. She profoundly impacted my life, and she was like a first-class angel to me. When my brother Ray read the first draft of the book, he said, "Franny, this isn't enough. You must make this bigger! I want more. You need to turn this into an advice book about life and love!"

I chuckled at Ray, and said, "Yeah, right!"

Ray persisted and said emphatically, "Franny, there are people out there who need to know about life and love, and you should write about it."

I said, "I would love to do that, but there's one problem. I can hardly be considered an authority. Did you forget, I'm getting divorced? I've failed in that area, don't you think?"

Ray said, "So what! Write about it anyway!"

Then he looked me in the eye and said, "You need to define love. 'What is love?' Don't tell one story, tell many stories about life and love. It will be great!"

I wrote down the conversation I had with Ray on the night that it took place. Every time I reread what he said, it helps me recall why I kept writing.

It was a hot summer night on the Fourth of July. Right after Ray told me to write an advice book that spoke about life and love, fireworks exploded in the sky. At that moment I felt a burst of excitement go off inside me. Even though I needed the advice of a love doctor myself, I felt as though I had just been commissioned by my brother to write a book that speaks about life and everything that hinges on its success: *LOVE!*

My original book went through many transformations. Finally, I decided to divide it into two books: This one, and the one that follows it, *Angel Melodies: The Ultimate Guide to Winning at Life & Love.*

If by chance you're hoping this is an advice book about marriage or romance, you'll find some "halo hints" and "winning tips" to assist in that way in this book, but you will find that much more in my second book, *Angel Melodies: The Ultimate Guide to Winning at Life & Love.*

Angel Melodies: The Little Guide to Winning at Life & Love at Any Stage of the Game has been written for a general audience. When you discover some of the easy ways that you can be a first-class angel and win at life and love, you will begin to experience greater joy and gratification, even if you are not married or in a romantic relationship.

You might be thinking: *Hold it right there. We're not angels; we're imperfect human beings.*

If that is what you're thinking, you are correct. We are humans, made up of flesh, blood, and many imperfections. However, a person who strives to be a channel of God's love operates as "God's special agent," or as I like to call them, "a first-class angel." Moreover, being a first-class angel to at least one person, a spouse, a child, a neighbor, or someone whose wing brushes up against ours for only one moment, is what makes us winners in life and love. We can also sense in our spirit when we are around a first-class angel. We feel happy, secure, and peaceful. I will share the first **halo hint** that will make it easier for you to operate as a first-class angel:

It is important to form friendships, partnerships, and alliances with other first-class angels and minimize the time that we spend with people who drag us down.

Girl Scout leaders always teach girl scouts the importance of the buddy system, where at least two or three girls watch out for each other. They are advised to warn each other of danger and never to leave the camp without at least one buddy. There is more than one scripture in the bible that tells us that two people working together, or journeying together, are better than one. Ecclesiastes 4:9, and Amos 3:3, to name only a few.

Luciano De Crescenzo said, "We are each of us angels, with only one wing, and we can only fly by embracing each other." Luciano is correct! We need people in our lives who operate as first-class angels to help us soar to a higher realm of love.

Whether you are married or single, it is important to carefully select friends who operate as first-class angels to accompany you and assist you on your life's journey. If you are single and longing to be married, ask the Lord to show you where you might find another first-class angel. Jesus promised us that if we seek, we will find. (Matthew 7:7)

Here are some Halo Hints to Help You Identify Other First-Class Angels:

- **First-class angels strive to be loving and tender-hearted.**

- **First-class angels are humble and kind.**

- **First-class angels do not play mind games.**

- **First-class angels tread lightly on people's emotions.**

- **First-class angels strive to be at peace with themselves and other people.**

- **First-class angels bring out the best in others.**

- **First-class angels defend the honor of others.**

- **First-class angels do not dwell on the faults of others and make light of people's faults.**

- **First-class angels inspire others to be first-class angels through their loving example.**

Bonus Halo Hint

A first-class angel deserves to marry another first-class angel. Otherwise, they are better off remaining single and having a lot of friends who are first-class angels.

The people I have known that have been first-class angels to me saw the best in me, and they looked out for my best interests. At times, they performed little acts of kindness that made my day a little easier or more enjoyable. Other times, they lavished me with their love. That's what I mean when I refer to a person as being a first-class angel.

I want to share a **halo hint** that is a direct quote from Mother Teresa:

"Let no one ever come to you without coming away better, happier. Be the living expression of God's kindness. Everybody should see kindness in your face, in your eyes, in your warm greeting."

Living as though we are one of the Missionaries of Charity is not an easy undertaking. However, it is a way of life that we can strive to live up to every day. There will be days when we will fail, but we can take a moment to remind ourselves that it is our job to help others to be happier and better off than what they were before their wing brushed up against our wing.

Always remember that our job as a first-class angel is to help people on their life's journey. We need to love them and do our best to protect them from physical and spiritual danger. Although we should not keep score, there should be a certain amount of give and take in our relationships. To subdue our natural inclination to be selfish, we need to strive to give more than we take.

You might be thinking; *I've been burned more than once while trying to be a nice person. I'm not sure that I want to operate as a first-class angel.*

If you were hurt recently, you might feel a need to place a protective barrier around yourself so you can heal. After you have had time to heal, it is important to keep in mind that it is easier to approach a person who does not have a protective wall around themselves. It is a lot easier to warm up to someone who can relate to our hardships because they have experienced some of their own difficulties. It is easier for us when a person does not come across as being a powerhouse or having a heart that has turned cold. What is easier for us, is easier for other people. We must remember the adage that our mothers taught us as children, "Treat others the way you want others to treat you."

If we want warmth, love, and compassion, we should give people warmth, love, and compassion. If deep in our hearts we want other people to approach us, we must show people that we are approachable no matter what hard knocks we have taken in life.

Do you need a little more convincing? Just pretend for a moment that the movie, "The Wizard of Oz," was based on a true story. Wasn't it a lot harder for Dorothy and her three friends to approach "The Great and Powerful Wizard of Oz" than it was for them to approach the humble and tender-hearted man that the wizard revealed himself to be after he came out from behind the curtain?

Most people are not any different than Dorothy, the scarecrow, the tin man, and the cowardly lion. Most of us would rather interact with a humble, kind, and tender-hearted person instead of a person who intimidates us or overpowers us. In the game of life and love, people who possess inner strength and a healthy amount of virtue attract more people. We must allow our hardships to soften us, rather than harden us.

When we interact with a stranger, who seems to be having a bad day, a warm smile and pleasant interaction with them will decrease their stress levels and help them to have a better day. **The ability to spread joy and diminish stress is the kind of power that first-class angels strive to possess.**

One of the problems with striving to be a first-class angel is that we make mistakes. When we're hurt, or we are stressed out, sometimes it is instinctive to lash out at someone. When we allow words to slip out of our mouth that offends a friend or a family member, we can apologize to them. If they allow us, we can try to reach out to them and give them a hug. We can fuss over them to regain their trust. It's important to go out of our way to make amends.

The Good Book tells us in 1 Peter 4:8 that love makes up for a multitude of sins. Even when we make mistakes, we retain our rank as first-class angels and continue to love God and the people God has placed on our path.

A Story of First-Class Angels

In my early forties, I went through a divorce. Shortly after, I met with a deacon at my church for spiritual direction to help me discern whether I should apply for an annulment. Even though I had five children with my former husband, the deacon believed that I should pursue it. One day after Mass the deacon took me to the side and said, "Francesca, I think you need to marry an Italian man."

I said, "Deacon, I know all about Italian men. They can be a little scary at times. I'd rather not marry an Italian man."

The Deacon said, "I still think you should marry an Italian man. So, I am going to tell you what I am going to do. I am going to pray that a man that is only half Italian will come into your life."

I laughed and said, "Okay, go ahead."

As I was working on my annulment and trying to write a new chapter of my life, the stress of being a single mother began to take a toll on me. I started experiencing adult-acne and rosacea. While I was at a prayer meeting one day, I noticed a woman with beautiful skin. Her skin was so smooth and flawless that she looked like an angel. I sighed and longed to have skin as beautiful as hers.

After the prayer meeting, the woman with the beautiful skin approached me and introduced herself to me as Veronica. She said, "I know you are newly divorced, and you have five children. I would love to give you a facial. I will only charge you twenty dollars, and I won't try to sell you any product. I think that you could use some TLC."

She handed me her business card. I thanked her and told her that I would think about it. A week or two later, I ended up with a huge, unsightly pimple on my cheek. I dug Veronica's card out of my purse and made an appointment.

The facial Veronica gave me was luxurious and soothing. After she gently washed and wrapped my face in a series of warm towels, I said, "I didn't know that a facial could be so relaxing and therapeutic. How long did it take you to become an esthetician?"

Veronica said, "If you go full time, it takes about a year. If you go part-time, it could take two years."

I said, "It sounds like something I would like to check into."

Veronica told me about some schools and encouraged me to check out their programs. About a month later, I enrolled in an esthetics school located up the street from my old high school. I learned that it is not only extremely relaxing to receive facials, but to give them as well. My acne and rosacea cleared up not only because of the products that we used at school but also because my stress levels diminished every time I gave or received a facial. Plus, the women at my school were a hoot. Laughter was the best medicine.

About a year later, my daughter took a picture of me. My skin was free of acne, and there was no flare-up of rosacea. I used the picture for my profile when I joined Catholic Match and ended up meeting a gentleman named Joe. One of the first things Joe told me was that he loved my picture because my face looked like it was glowing. We messaged each other a few times and spoke on the phone a few times. One day Joe said, "How would you feel about meeting a man who has been out of work for a year and is living with his mother?"

I laughed and said, "I don't have a job either. I'm going to school in the hope of starting a new career. The economy has been bad for a while. Millions of people are unemployed. Hmm, a grown man living with his mother? It sounds like something an Italian guy would do. Are you by any chance Italian?"

Joe said, "I am half Italian."

I said, "Really? I'm a hundred percent Italian. Are you, by any chance, half Irish too?"

Joe said, "No, I'm half Polish."

I said, "Darn. I was hoping that you were half Irish. I love the way the Irish place a lot of value on love, loyalty, and friendship."

Joe said, "You don't have to be Irish to value love, loyalty, and friendship. I would love to meet you in person."

I said, "I'd love to be your tour guide when you come to Chicago."

Joe flew into Chicago a few weeks later. We were both pleasantly surprised to learn that there was a Celtic festival taking place at Millennial Park in downtown Chicago the weekend that he came to town. We had a great time at the festival. Joe gained a new appreciation for Irish music and traditions.

A couple of weeks after we met, a plant manager position became available about forty miles from my house. Joe interviewed for the job, and he got it. A week or two later Joe gave me an Irish Claddagh ring and pledged his love, loyalty, and friendship to me! A few years later, we got married. The deacon was invited to our wedding, and he provided us with an Irish blessing.

If the Deacon had not planted a seed in my mind that I should marry an Italian guy and had not told me that he was going to pray that a half Italian man would come into my life, I might not have recognized a good thing when it was happening. Joe came on strong when he pledged his love, loyalty, and friendship to me after only knowing me for a short time. It was a little scary diving headfirst into a relationship. I accepted the ring and decided to allow Joe to prove his love, loyalty, and friendship to me.

Scripture tells us in 1 John 4:1 that we "must prove the spirit." When we are considering marriage, we must give a person enough time to prove to us that they are truly operating as a first-class angel. After dating Joe for about two years, he passed every test with flying colors. I married Joe because he loved me as described in 1 Corinthians 13:4-6, the scripture passage often used at weddings. Joe continues to love me as described in the "love is" scripture passage.

If Veronica had not approached me to give me a facial, I might not have gone to esthetics school. My rosacea and acne would have remained the same. My daughter would not have been able to take a picture of me with my skin aglow. I would not have had an attractive picture to place on a dating website. Going back to school also boosted my self-confidence, enough to help me enter the dating scene once again. Veronica's act of kindness had a powerful impact on my personal and professional life.

If you can recognize how the deacon, Veronica, Maria, and Joe operated as first-class angels and the ways they impacted my life, I believe you have been called to operate as a first-class angel and soar to a higher realm of love.

As you read the stories about other first-class angels in this book and see how they are winning the game of life and love, God is going to reveal to you the ways that He wants you to operate as a first-class angel and be a winner in the game of life and love!

Although this is an advice book, I am not suggesting that you change any aspect of your life or that you follow the flight patterns of the first-class angels in this book. The stories of the first-class angels are intended to serve only as a source of inspiration to you. What you can expect as you read this book is that you're going to admire some of the qualities of the first-class angels. By the time you're finished reading this book, some of the qualities of the first-class angels will rub off on you and bring out the good that already exists in you!

Many of the stories in this book will appeal to women. Some of them will appeal to men. I love the title and cover of this book, but I don't know how many men are going to crack open a book entitled *Angel Melodies.* If you're a woman who has a son, brother, boyfriend, or husband who might benefit from reading this book, I ask you to recommend the book to him or that you read some chapters of this book to him. You might be the only way that I will be able to deliver an important message to a man who needs to hear it. When you serve as the message carrier, you will be operating as a first-class angel just like the deacon, when he delivered a very important message to me!

God wants us to win the game of life and love by receiving God's love and sharing God's love with others. As first-class angels, we have an important mission for our life here on Earth! **Our main mission is to create a little piece of Heaven on Earth in our neck of the woods!**

Most of the people I have written about in my books had no idea there was a love paparazzi on the watch, taking pictures of them with her heart, writing about their expressions of love in not just one, but two books.

The stories that I share in my books are designed not only to inspire but to motivate you and me to be the kind of loving person the Lord wants us to be. When we form the habit of giving and receiving love, it becomes a lot easier for us to wake up every morning and feel as though we have what it takes to win the game of life and love!

I chose the name "Angel Melodies" for multiple reasons. For one, my dear friend, who I fondly refer to as "Angela" in my books played the part of a first-class angel when we were in a grade school play together. Secondly, she was like an angel who saw the best in me and watched out for me when we were kids. Lastly, there have been times after her death when it seemed like she was an angel looking over my shoulder watching out for me once again. If it hadn't been for my cherished memories of my childhood friend, I never would have written more than one book that speaks about the importance of being a first-class angel. She was the inspiration for both of my books. Angela has some small parts in this book. However, she is one of the main characters in my other book entitled *Angel Melodies: The Ultimate Guide to Winning at Life & Love.*

Many of my fondest memories are like angel melodies to me in that they tug at my heartstrings, thanks to my children and all the first-class angels who have loved my family and me during the high notes and low notes of life. I hope the stories about the first-class angels contained in this book will tug at your heartstrings too!

Instructions for This Book

One of the ways I would like to assist you in maintaining or bettering your relationships is by providing you with "halo hints" which serve as "winning tips." Just as you did in this chapter, you will find halo hints scattered throughout the upcoming chapters.

The halo hints are designed to inspire you to operate as a first-class angel. In this book, you're also going to find a reference to a song in many of the chapters. The songs are "angel melodies" that will assist you in winning the game of life and love. I will ask you to look up the songs and take a music break to listen and reflect on them. Don't skip this very important step because the songs will touch your heart, help you to soar to a higher realm of love, and provide you with the winner's edge.

When my children were not old enough to read, I directed a Nativity play for them to perform with some of my nieces and nephews for our family. I made costumes for them, and they looked as precious as sweet, little angels. I had a children's storybook that told the story of Jesus' birth that I used for our little Christmas production. What was unique about the children's storybook was that it had musical buttons on the side of the book that played the melodies of Christmas carols to correspond with the story of the Nativity. During our Nativity play, I read the book out loud while my children and some of my nieces and nephews played their silent parts as Mother Mary, Saint Joseph, Baby Jesus, the shepherds, and the Magi. When I pushed the musical button on the side of the book, the adults began singing the Christmas carols that corresponded with the story of Jesus's birth. Everybody had a wonderful time that tugged at their heartstrings. Everybody experienced joy and felt the Lord's presence when they participated in the play.

The Christmas songs made the characters of the Nativity story come to life for us as we sang along and interacted with the little children. I would like you to have an interactive experience with this book by listening to the songs that I ask you to look up. If you are willing to pull a few of your own heartstrings with the use of music listening, this book will have much more meaning for you.

CHAPTER 2

Wrestling with Life & Death

My friend Angela's greatest concern when she was dying was that her life was not going to matter to anybody. She was only thirty years old when she was facing death. Her two children were very young. One of them was a newborn.

Angela's husband was a successful, tall, dark, handsome man with big broad shoulders and a dynamic personality. I wasn't the least bit surprised that Angela fell head over heels, madly in love with Troy. When we were kids, she always told me that one day she wanted to marry a very handsome man, live in a big, beautiful house, and have two beautiful children – a boy and a girl. Her life went exactly as she had hoped and dreamed. Unfortunately, she was unable to "live the dream" for very long.

As she was facing death, she was plagued by the unknown and concerned about things she wouldn't be able to control after she was gone. She knew the moment she died that her husband would become an eligible bachelor. Moreover, their two beautiful children would serve as her husband's wing angels to tug at the heartstrings of many women. Angela was afraid that after her husband got remarried that his memory of her would fade away, and it would be as though she never existed, especially in the lives of her two children.

That concern weighed heavily on her mind the very last time we spoke to each other a few weeks before she passed away. I did not want her mind going to a dark place. I told her that her life would continue to matter to all the people who loved her, and we would share our memories of her with her children.

At the time, I was a new mother myself. I had a beautiful baby girl who had just turned one year old. I had no idea what it must have been like for my dear friend to wrap her mind around the sad reality of leaving her family behind when the doctors told her there was nothing more they could do to help her, except to make her feel as comfortable as possible.

However, what I did understand as a new mother was the major sacrifices that are necessary for any woman to bring a child into the world. I knew, without a shadow of a doubt, that my friend's children wouldn't have had a life to live if it hadn't been for their mother's loving sacrifice. Therefore, her life did matter, and it would always matter for all eternity. She changed the course of history by bringing not just one, but two beautiful children into the world. There is no greater way for a woman to have an impact on the world than to bring a child into the world. As a mother, I also believe a child is our hope for the future, even if every mother died tomorrow.

I believed then, and I believe now that my friend has always been a part of her children. There is something to be said for possessing the same DNA as one's parents. I believe the saying, "blood is thicker than water," holds water. It would not be surprising if Angela's son and daughter ended up taking after their mother in a variety of ways, even though her children were very small when she held them in her arms the very last time.

As for my friend and me, we were such close friends that she became a part of who I am as well, so much so that I feel as though we share the same DNA. That's why I promised myself that I would write about her life after she died. I wanted to honor her life by sharing my loving memories, one day when the time was right.

Not too long ago, my friend's son contacted me on Facebook as a full-grown adult. He said he heard that I had written a book about his mother, and he asked me if he could read it. I tried to reach out to him by sending a friend request several months before. However, I did not hear from him until I was at a hospital in Chicago dealing with my son's medical crisis. My son was beginning his long journey toward recovery. The message from my deceased friend's son made me feel as though my friend had found a way to reach out to me, even though I could not see the shadow of her ghost. Though so many years had passed since her death, I felt Angela was there for me when I needed her friendship, love, and compassion.

For now, I am happy to say that my friend didn't have to worry her pretty, little heart out that she would soon be forgotten. Her son, who was about three years old when his mother passed away, never forgot about his mother.

CHAPTER 3

Momma Bird Flies from the Nest

In the first chapter, I said that a first-class angel deserves to marry another first-class angel. However, there is one proviso that I did not mention up front. Sometimes a first-class angel must widen their search, spread their wings, and fly to a distant land to be with another first-class angel!

Initially, Joe moved from Pensacola, Florida, to the Chicago area to spend time with me. After we had been dating for two years, his job took him to New Orleans. Six months later, I tearfully asked my three oldest children for their blessing to marry Joe and move nine hundred miles away from home.

Charley said, "Mom, I told you before Joe moved away that you should marry him. You're not going to find a guy who treats you better. I don't want to hurt your feelings or anything, but I have always wanted the chance to live with Dad."

Tommy said, "Mom, I only have one year left of high school. I've always wanted the chance to live with Dad too."

Maria said, "Mom, you know that I think you should marry Joe. He's a great guy. Just pretend that you're going on a vacation. You two might be able to move back here one day. Somehow, we'll figure out a way to be together again."

I was relieved, but not surprised when Maria, Tommy, and Charley gave me their blessing. My three older children had never been clingy. On the day they left for preschool, they did not shed any tears. They gained an additional sense of independence when they got a job. They gained more independence when they got their driver's license. They took a flying leap of independence when they got a set of wheels. After my kids had their three ducks lined up in a row, they came home briefly only to refuel. Then they flew out the door again.

When I migrated to the South, my two oldest sons didn't seem to need me. It was apparent that they wanted and needed to spend more time bonding with their father before they made their full transition into adulthood. Maria was a busy college student.

The song, "I Will Always Love You," written by Dolly Parton, which was made popular by Whitney Houston, describes how I felt when I flew from the nest. Let's take a little music break to listen to it.

Although I had spent much of my life playing it safe, there was a spirit of adventure that had been locked inside of me that needed to be set free as well. From the time I was a child, I wanted to be like my great-grandmother, Francesca.

Francesca was born in Sicily around the year 1880. She was a free-spirit who was not afraid to follow her heart. When she was a young woman, she started a new adventure by slipping love notes to a man named Peter who worked in her father's shoe store. Another employee saw Francesca slipping a love note to Peter. Rumors started circulating in Agrigento. Forward behavior of a young woman in those days was considered risqué.

Francesca had a privileged upbringing, and her parents already arranged for their daughter to marry a man from a prominent family. Her parents were aghast when they learned that their daughter initiated a relationship with an unrefined hired-hand. When Francesca ran off with Peter against her parents' wishes and immigrated to the United States, she forfeited her inheritance.

After the newly wedded couple arrived by ship on Ellis Island, Francesca and Peter made their way to Chicago and rented a small studio apartment. When they first set up house, their furniture was constructed of orange crates that they found on the side of the road. Many years later Francesca told her children that if her mother had seen her living conditions when she arrived in Chicago that her mother would have wept bitterly. Francesca also said that she was very happy even though she and Peter had always lived on nothing but love.

Some of Francesca's friends told her as a young bride that she was married to the most handsome man in America. To maintain a hedge of protection around her marriage, Francesca was generous with her affection. She conceived a baby fourteen times and gave birth to nine children.

During her life, she believed that each baby that she carried in her womb was far more precious than all the wealth in the world. For that reason, she regarded herself as an extremely wealthy woman. Peter died in his fifties. Francesca lived to her eighties and died two months before I was born.

As a teenage girl, I was told by my Grandmother that her parents never acquired any wealth, but instead possessed a richness in their relationship that many married couples never acquire. I have carried my great-grandparents love story inside my heart since the time I was a young child. When I was a half-century old, I wanted to follow my heart, embark on a new adventure, and give love a fighting chance. I also wanted to send a message to my five children that it is good to spread our wings and explore uncharted territory. I knew my children would feel freer to spread their wings and embark on their own adventure one day because of my willingness to fly from the nest.

It is one thing to want to be a free spirit and to want to be a person who follows one's heart. It's an entirely different ball game to be that kind of person. Taking on a spirited initiative isn't an easy endeavor when a woman has several children. Moreover, it's instinctive for a mother to want to continue acting like a mother hen even when her children are independent and want to take of themselves.

A big part of me wanted to remain with all my children until all of them were ready to fly from the nest. The other part of me wanted to spread my wings and fly south to be with Joe. My heart was torn.

While Joe and I were dating, I had an ideal living arrangement with my children. I rented a house located across the street from a Catholic Church. I loved the location, and my children loved it too. It was easy for me to go to Mass or run over to church to say a few prayers whenever my children tested me. The lights of the church lit up two entryways of my house until eleven o'clock at night. My children knew that I wanted them home before the church lights went out. Living a stone's throw from a church made me feel as though my children and I had extra guardian angels watching over us. My older children were able to walk to school and their father's fitness center.

I'm spontaneous and enjoy flying by the seat of my pants, except when I am looking for a new place to nest. I've learned not only from what I have read but also from personal experience that location is everything. Joe thought I would feel at home in New Orleans because there is a high percentage of Catholics. He scouted out more than one suburb before I visited him. As we drove down River Road in Destrehan, my eyes were drawn to Saint Charles Borromeo Catholic Church. Its Old-World charm stood out to me along with its white stucco, white columns, and white arches. The burnt orange Spanish tiles covering the roof of the church reminded me of Angela and her husband. When they got married, they embarked on an adventure together when they moved from Illinois to California. Troy, with his magnetic personality and charm, practically struck gold selling Spanish tile roofing on the west coast. I also admired Angela for having been a free-spirit. When she was young and in love, she had no problem following her heart.

Joe knew that I was willing to consider a move to Louisiana but that I had no desire to live there long-term. To make my decision to marry him easier, he promised that we would spend time exploring many parts of the country. Then we would decide together where we would live during retirement.

I told Joe that I had a feeling before I met him that I would one day move to the South. I pictured myself living in South Carolina or Georgia, near a lake or a golden pond. I had a hard time picturing myself living in the deeper depths of the South when Joe gave me the grand tour of the swamps!

I loved Chicago and was accustomed to a glamorous city with beautiful skyscrapers, a gold coast, and a Magnificent Mile. For the love of Joe and for the sake of keeping our love story alive, I was trying to keep an open mind about moving to NOLA. The struggle was real! The thought of living in or near a city that is threatened by seasonal hurricanes and is sinking into the Gulf of Mexico was not my idea of a fairytale. It was nightmarish!

Next to Saint Charles Borromeo Church in Destrehan was a cemetery with above ground tombs. My thoughts drifted back to my high school days when Angela and our friends used to go on joy rides from our neck of the woods to Saint James Church. It was one of the oldest Catholic churches in the Chicago area. This church was known as "Monk's Castle." There was a cemetery there too, and a little monastery which served as the dwelling place for the pastor and some monks. A few times, we parked our cars in the entryway just outside a huge wrought-iron, black gate. Then we jumped out of our cars and ran up a steep hill which led us to the cemetery with the intent to scare the living daylights out of ourselves.

It upset the monks when they heard us screaming at the top of our lungs as we ran up, and just as quickly, down the hill as fast as our legs would take us. More than once, the monks ran out of the monastery, chased after us, and shouted at us to get off the property. With their black robes and hoodies, it was as though they were zombie ghosts risen from the dead. We pulled off that prank only a few times before the monks decided to lock the gate at night to prevent us from waking up the actual dead!

While driving down River Road in Destrehan, I spotted a bike path on top of a levee which separated us from the Mississippi River. I suspected that Joe took me sightseeing down that road because he knew that I love bike paths. It was easy for me to envision Joe, Johnny, Tony, and I riding our bikes along that Mississippi River bike trail.

As Joe drove a little further up River Road, I also saw an enormous white building which reminded me of the White House in DC. Joe told me that it was a mansion that was owned by Jesse Duplantis, an Evangelical Christian minister.

Behind Jesse's mansion was an upscale neighborhood. A little further down River Road was a quaint middle-class neighborhood. As we were driving through the middle-class neighborhood, Joe pointed out that many children were playing outside.

Joe said, "It would be good if we lived in a neighborhood that has a lot of children. It would make the transition easier for Johnny and Tony."

I said, "I'd like Johnny and Tony to have the opportunity to play outside with a big group of kids. This area seems to have more than one redeeming quality. I hope this town has some nice grocery stores and delis close by."

Joe said, "I gave you my old smartphone over a month ago. Have you tried to use it yet? You could check it out on your phone."

I said, "Sorry, I still have not figured this thing out. Could you pull over for a minute, and show me how to use it?"

Joe pulled over and said, "Ok, all you have to do is push the round button, and hold it there for a second until the phone asks you, 'What can I help you with?' Good. There you go. Now speak to the phone by saying 'grocery stores.'"

I did what Joe told me to do and spoke to a smartphone for the first time in my life. The phone said, "Ok Francesca. Here's what I found."

I said, "It looks like there is a Winn Dixie about a mile away. I already know that's not gourmet. There's also a Walmart that isn't anywhere near here. Any chance we might find a good Italian deli?"

Joe smiled and said, "All you have to do is check your smartphone."

I pushed the round button again and said, "Delis."

The phone said, "It looks like there is a Subway not too far from here."

I rolled my eyes at Joe and said, "Subway. That's it? You want me to move to a place that doesn't have any good grocery stores or delis?"

Joe said, "New Orleans is known for its muffuletta. It's a round sub sandwich stuffed with Italian meats and cheeses. It comes with a spicy olive salad that is like Italian giardiniera.

I said, "Why do they call it Muffuletta? Muffa is an Italian term my Aunt Agnes uses to describe the smell of mildew. There is mildew everywhere around here. It's bad enough that we can see the muffa and smell the muffa. Do we have to eat it too?"

Joe said, "I don't know why they call it Muffuletta. Have you ever eaten blue cheese? It has mildew in it too. I spotted a farmer's market back on River Road. Do you want to go there? One of the vendors might be selling muffuletta. I'd like you to try it."

I said, "Oh Joe, now you're speaking my love language. Just what I've always wanted... to have my mildew, and to eat it too."

Joe said, "That's a good one. You're funny."

I said, "I'm not trying to be funny. Do you love me or are you trying to kill me by forcing me to eat a mildew sandwich? What's next on the agenda? Are you going to dump my dead body into the Mississippi River?"

Joe said, "Sweetie, I love you, and I would never do anything to hurt you. I want to marry you and love you like Christ loves the Church."

I said, "Are you saying that you love me so much that you would die for me if it were necessary?"

Joe said, "Yes, I would die for you if it were necessary."

I said, "You are such a prince charming. Now you really are speaking my love language. Speaking of love languages, have you ever read the book called "The Five Love Languages?"

Joe said, "Yes. I read it from cover to cover."

I said, "I wonder why Gary Chapman said there are only five love languages. I think there are a lot more."

Joe said, "What would you add to the list of love languages?

I said, "When we pray together, I feel very close to you. I also feel like you are speaking one of my love languages."

Joe said, "I feel very close to you when we pray too. I don't remember if Gary Chapman covered the topic of prayer. It's been a while since I read the book."

I said, "Would you like to read "The Five Love Languages" with me?"

Joe said, "Whatever makes you happy."

I said, "I do not think Gary mentioned anything about dancing together or singing together in the car. Expressing love for each other in those ways allows a couple to be more in sync with each other. If two people aren't in sync with each other, it throws their entire relationship out of whack."

Joe said, "Hmm. I never thought about it that way."

I said, "I think married couples from the 1940s and 1950s had a low divorce rate because they danced together and spent much of their time learning how to be in sync with each other before they got married."

Joe said, "I enjoy slow dancing with you."

I said, "Slow dancing and swaying to the music is nice, but I enjoy twirling as they did back in the 1950s."

Joe said, "If you want, we can take some dance lessons together."

I said, "Now you're speaking my love language."

Joe said, "Okay, it's my turn to add a love language to the list. I know that cooking with love and sharing a good meal is one of your love languages."

I said, "I enjoy cooking with love. Do you want to know who said cooking and sharing a meal is a way to say, 'I love you?'"

Joe said, "Somebody on the cooking channel?"

I said, "It was Mr. Rogers. He sang a song called, 'Many Ways to Say I Love You.' I used to sing it to my children when they were little. Mr. Rogers said that loving people and animals are one of the most important parts of being alive. I love people and animals, but I also think cooking with love is one of the most important parts of being alive."

Joe said, "If it is that important to you, I think we should also take a cooking class together."

I said, "I'd love to take some dancing and cooking classes with you, but do we have to take them in New Orleans? Does your company have a branch in another part of the country? It is crazy how hot and humid it is here."

Joe said, "Sweetie, that's why there is air-conditioning. If you can't handle the heat and humidity, we'll stay inside where it's cooler."

I said, "If I moved here, every day would be a bad hair day."

Joe said, "You would look pretty even if you wore a babushka.

I said, "The only way I would wear a babushka is if we were driving in a convertible with the top down in a place where we could enjoy the weather, and we pretended to be Elvis and Priscilla Presley."

Joe said, "That sounds like fun. We can rent a convertible when we go on our honeymoon."

I said, "Joe, I don't think you understand how much you're asking of me. If I moved here, I would feel like I am a foreigner in a foreign country!"

Joe said, "New Orleans is a melting pot of a lot of people originally from Old World countries. It isn't any different than Chicago."

I said, "Even though Chicago is a melting pot of people originally from Old World countries, for some reason Chicago is more modernized than New Orleans."

Joe said, "If anybody should be able to deal with a lack of modernization it should be you. Your brothers say that you are a flashback of the 1950s."

I said, "Joe, I was hoping that if we got married that you would help me to be a modern woman. I didn't think you would stick me in a time machine and send me back even further in time."

Joe said, "I know that asking you to move here is asking a lot of you, but I need to explain something to you. I just want you to know that I learned with my line of work that there is always a reason that God takes me to a new job or an entirely new state. A couple of years ago, I didn't understand why it was taking so long for me to find another job after I was laid off. Then I met you on Catholic Match, and a month later a good job opened for me in Chicago. You were the reason God brought me to Chicago.

"There were other times when I did not understand the reason God moved me from one location to the other. After I lived in a place for a while, I started to understand why God uprooted me and sent me to a new place. Now I don't understand why God took me away from Chicago and brought me to New Orleans. I trust that sooner or later, God will show me."

I said, "Joe, you are accustomed to moving. You have learned how to make any place your home. I have lived in the same place my whole life. I am accustomed to having four seasons. I like the snow. Snow is very pretty."

Joe said, "Snow is pretty until it turns black just like mildew around here. Francesca, I don't want to live here any more than you do, but I would enjoy living here a lot more if you were here with me. I told you when we first met that I enjoy being a family man. Two of my children are adults, and my youngest daughter lives with her mother. I believe we were meant to be together. I want to help you finish raising your two younger sons. Your older children are more independent than a lot of kids their age, and they have given you their blessing to marry me.

"Let's address the most important issue. It's not the climate or the culture in New Orleans that is holding you back from marrying me; it's leaving your three older children and your other family members in Chicago."

I said, "Yes, you're right. I always pictured myself being the matriarch of my family. I feel like I would be giving up an important part of my life by moving far away from my children. If we could live somewhere in between my relatives and your relatives, it would be better for everybody. My family and your family would be more inclined to visit us, especially during the holidays."

Joe said, "I have a feeling, we will have to visit our families during the holidays no matter where we live. Our families are used to their traditions. The most important issue that remains is that you are going to miss your three older children and your other family members if you marry me and move away."

I said, "Yes, I would miss my children and my family! Do you want to know what's even more upsetting? I don't know that they would miss me! When I asked my family for their blessing to marry you, it felt like everybody was trying to get rid of me!"

Joe said, "That's even more reason that you should marry me. I miss you like crazy. You know Maria will miss you, but she is in college and has a heavy school load. She leads a busy life. Tommy and Charley also have busy lives and would probably appreciate you a lot more after you moved away.

"The rest of your family loves you. They aren't trying to get rid of you. Everybody wants you and me to get married because they know we are good for each other. After we get married, we will drive back to Chicago and Pensacola as often as we can to see our children and our family. We'll just have to learn how to be road warriors."

Halo Hint

Communication is an essential part of a first-class angel's job description. Good communication is like a bridge that draws people closer together. To win the game of life and love, a first-class angel must do their best to be a good communicator!

Joe pulled the car back onto River Road. Just down the road from Jesse's mansion was Destrehan Plantation. Right next door to the plantation was the farmer's market located on an empty lot. As soon as we got out of the car, we could hear a man singing love songs from the 1950s. It seemed like the love songs were beckoning me to marry Joe and move to Destrehan, Louisiana.

On that note, I would like to dedicate a song to my husband, Joe. It's called "You're Nobody 'Til Somebody Loves You" with Dean Martin.

CHAPTER 4

First-Class Angels in Training

During the second semester of her sophomore year in college, Maria moved into her aunt and uncle's house. She enjoyed staying with her aunt and uncle for a year and a half. When her grandfather passed away during Maria's last semester of college, she moved in with her grandmother to lift her grandma's spirits. Maria spent most of her time in the library at college, but her grandmother truly appreciated any time that they spent together. Maria's desire to lift the spirit of a person who has experienced a great loss is one of the qualities that makes my daughter a first-class angel, and a winner at the game of life and love.

Halo Hint

Being someone who tries to lift a person's spirits and be a support beam when they are broken-hearted is a beautiful quality of a first-class angel.

My son, Tommy, was entering his senior in high school when I moved away. From the time Tommy was a young child, he felt a strong call to join the military. He possesses a lot of patriotism and love for our country. After he serves in the military, he wants to become a physical therapist.

Halo Hint

Patriotism, a strong desire to serve others, and protect one's country are noble qualities of a first-class angel.

My son, Charley, was entering his junior year in high school when I moved away. Just like his older siblings, he excelled in math and science. He still had time to decide which college he wanted to attend. He was taking a heavy load of challenging classes with the hope that he would get into any college.

Charley also had his own lawn-care business. After he started working, he stopped asking his father and me for money. He started working at fourteen years old because he got weary of playing monkey in the middle.

Charley said, "Whenever I went to my mother for money, she would say, 'Go to your father, he's got all the money.' Whenever I went to my father and asked for money, he would say, 'Go to your mother, she's got all the money.' I got tired of dealing with my parents, so I decided to make my own money."

As soon as Charley turned sixteen, he bought a pickup truck from the money that he made cutting lawns during his early career. He also purchased second-hand industrial lawn-care equipment. Charley enjoyed sharing prosperity with his friends. He helped them make money by providing them with opportunities to work with him.

Halo Hint

Providing others with a good financial opportunity is an outstanding quality of a first-class angel. It also builds the economy!

Johnny and Tony were not just good sports. They were great sports. They never complained when I got married to Joe, uprooted their lives, and moved them to Louisiana.

Halo Hint

Going with the flow is a great quality of a first-class angel.

Although it was not easy for me to leave my three older children in Chicago, I knew they already had what it took to operate as first-class angels. My children are living proof that you're never too young to start operating as a first-class angel. My children are also living proof that kids could turn out alright, even when they do not have perfect parents or an ideal childhood--with the proviso that they have at least one praying parent and other prayer warriors in their corner.

Prayer draws God's protection and mercy upon us and our family members. The more people that take their prayer life seriously, the better it is for our family, our country, and the world. When one prayer warrior goes to heaven, other family members must pick up the prayer torch and keeping the fire of love burning before the Lord.

Halo Hint

Praying for our family and friends and being a candle in the darkness are important aspects of a first-class angel's job description.

On that note, let's take another music break to listen to Debbie Boone sing, "You Light Up My Life."

CHAPTER 5

The Welcoming Angels

Joe, Johnny, Tony and I arrived in Destrehan, Louisiana, on the 2012 Fourth of July weekend. Even though it was unbearably hot and humid, Johnny and Tony spent many hours playing outside with their new friends in the neighborhood on the first day of our arrival.

The following weekend, I passed up an invitation to attend a crawfish boil at a neighbor's house. Johnny and Tony accepted the invitation. When they came home that evening, they told me how much they loved crawfish. I crinkled my nose in disgust.

A few days later the same neighbor who invited our family to the crawfish boil came to my house, carrying a small plate of homemade crawfish pies. I bit into one and told Lynette that I enjoyed the crawfish wrapped in a little pastry, but I was not so sure that I would enjoy eating them out of the shell.

Lynette said, "I know it is going to take a while for you to get used to living in Louisiana, but I think you're going to love Mardi Gras."

When Mardi Gras came along eight months later, Lynette invited us to attend more than one parade with her family and friends. She was kind enough to make more than one attempt to welcome my family and me to Louisiana. Lynette is a first-class angel and a winner at the game of life and love who understands the importance of welcoming newcomers.

Halo Hint

The ability to welcome newcomers is a beautiful quality of a first-class angel.

My sons had the time of their lives the first summer of our arrival in Destrehan but were disappointed when school began the second week of August.

A few months later, my boys were overjoyed when school let out for the entire week of Thanksgiving. We were happy to learn that Christmas break was longer than what we were accustomed to as Northerners. We were also pleasantly surprised when school let out once again for the entire week of Mardi Gras. The kids had yet another week off for Easter. The school year ended in the middle of May.

I loved the school schedule in New Orleans and thought every school district in the United States should be on the same schedule. Our ability to take frequent mini-trips and vacations was the biggest advantage of living in a suburb of NOLA. It allowed my children and me to adapt to a Cajun-Creole lifestyle without getting too homesick. We took many road trips to Chicago and Pensacola to see our families.

Joe was right; God always sends him somewhere to work for an important reason. I believe the main reason God allowed Joe to work in New Orleans for two years was to make it easier for the four of us to see our family in Chicago and Pensacola. We placed a lot of mileage on our minivan those first two years, but it was worth it. It is amazing how God gave Johnny, Tony and me the vacation time that we needed when I married Joe and moved nine hundred miles away from family. Another blessing was that Johnny and Tony made some very good friends in Destrehan, Louisiana, and they loved living there. The transition was easier for them than it was for me.

Another blessing of living in southern Louisiana is the early arrival of spring. Tulips and daffodils pop up as early as Valentine's Day. Azaleas, irises, lilies, and many other flowers blossom as early as March. The first time I plucked a magnolia from a tree, it reminded me that the story I had been writing about my friend Angela had some similarities to the movie, *Steel Magnolias*.

Right when I was getting used to living in southern Louisiana, Joe's job took us to the northwest corner of Louisiana. Some people call it, "Eastern Texas." It was easy for me to adjust to life in Benton, Louisiana.

The farmlands and rolling-meadows reminded me of some places I had lived in Illinois.

Joe suggested that I volunteer at a church to get to know some people. I volunteered to answer phones at Saint Jude Catholic Church. I told the pastor's secretary that I was writing a book that was the Yankee version of *Steel Magnolias*. I was surprised when the words rolled off my tongue. It was the first time I had ever described one of my books as the Yankee version of *Steel Magnolias* to anyone.

Peggy said, "It's funny that you're writing the Yankee version of *Steel Magnolias*, and now you live in the *Steel Magnolia* state."

I said, "What are you talking about Peggy?"

Peggy said, "Francesca, don't you know that *Steel Magnolias* is based on a true-life story that took place right here in Louisiana?"

I said, "I knew the movie took place in the South, but I didn't know it is based on a true-life story or that it took place in Louisiana. Where in Louisiana?"

Peggy said, "In Natchitoches, about seventy miles south of here."

I said, "I can't believe that I am that close to the home of *Steel Magnolias*. The colors at my wedding were pink and pink, just like Shelby's in *Steel Magnolias*. Shelby selected shades of pink that were blush and bashful. I selected shades of pink that were vibrant and not so bashful."

Peggy chuckled and said, "I still can't believe you didn't know that *Steel Magnolias* is based on a true-life story that took place here in Louisiana. I thought it was common knowledge."

I said, "Not to me. I'm so happy that you told me. I will visit Natchitoches and pay close attention to the details the next time I watch the movie."

Peggy said, "Now that you are here, we are not going to let you go. You belong to Saint Jude Church, and this is your home. Since God also blessed you with a beautiful home, would you be willing to host a Christmas party for the front-desk volunteers?"

I said, "My house is designed for family gatherings, but I don't have enough family here to gather. I would love to host a Christmas party for the front-desk volunteers. It would make it a lot easier for me to make new friends."

Later, I learned that Peggy grew up in Natchitoches. That is why she understood the historical and geographical background *of Steel Magnolias*. Peggy is a first-class angel and winner at life and love who provided me with an opportunity to make new friends in Louisiana.

Halo Hint

A willingness to help someone to make new friends is a beautiful quality of a first-class angel.

Not only was Peggy operating as a first-class angel when she asked me to have the Christmas Party, she unknowingly served as God's messenger. Before having the conversation with Peggy about *Steel Magnolias*, I had asked God many times why He brought me to Louisiana. If given an option to live anywhere in the

South, Louisiana is not a place I would have selected. However, my special connection with *Steel Magnolias* seems to be one of the reasons God brought me to Louisiana. More mind-blowing to me is knowing that after Joe retires, it will be difficult for me to leave Louisiana. I will miss the easy-going way of life, the beautiful scenery, and the wonderful people I have embraced as friends and family in Louisiana more than anything.

Since I left Chicago, some of my family members and some of my children have moved to other parts of the country. For now, Chicago remains our hub where many of my family members still come together to refill our love tanks.

Halo Hint

A first-class angel must be willing to go the distance not just for "the one we love" but also for the "ones we love."

I am grateful that my mother always welcomes me into her home with open arms and allows me to entertain my family and friends at her home when I am in Chicago. My mother tries to take things in stride and does not get too upset with the chaos that I bring to her life. We eat, drink, talk, laugh and make merry.

My mother still makes lasagna a couple of times a year for special occasions. Each lasagna weighs about twenty pounds. She also shares old family recipes and provides cooking lessons for her grandchildren when they visit her. When my mom came to visit me in Louisiana, she insisted that we attempt to make southern fried chicken instead of purchasing KFC. These are no small undertakings because my mother is in her eighties. She is living proof that a person is never too old to operate as a first-class angel!

Halo Hint

A willingness to make sacrifices for the love of family and friends at any stage of the game is a beautiful quality of a first-class angel.

CHAPTER 6

How to Mend a Rift

Before I married Joe and moved to Louisiana, my daughter Maria was attending a college in a western suburb of Chicago. It was close to our home, but I wanted Maria to experience life on a college campus because it was something that I never experienced. Maria lived on the college campus for one year, until we figured out that it wasn't worth the added drama or the expense.

Shortly after I became a licensed esthetician, I decided to provide Maria and some of her college friends with a spa-day. I packed up my lotions and potions, and I brought them to Maria's dorm. I enjoyed pampering them and advising them about what they needed to do to maintain their youthful appearance.

I was so happy that my daughter was living the dream with her college friends. Daughter was happy, and Mother was happy too.

Maria always came home on Sunday morning to go to church with her brothers and me. Then we would go out to eat for breakfast, and she would tell me about the drama that was taking place in the dorm.

One day I said to Maria, "I think you're having trouble getting along with the girls in your dorm because females tend to compete with other females. Look at Grandma Fran and Aunt Agnes. It seemed like Grandma Fran was always trying to compete with her older sister. When I was growing up my mom would get upset because her house was not as well-kept as Aunt Agnes's house. Grandma Fran used to turn into a lunatic the day before a party, trying to get our house to look party-perfect. The person Grandma felt the need to impress the most was her older sister because Aunt Agnes is persnickety when it comes to cleanliness. Everybody knows that she is the cleanliness goddess of our family and that cleanliness is next to goddess-li-ness.

"One day, Grandma Fran finally outshined Aunt Agnes when everybody said her lasagna was the best lasagna anybody had ever tasted at one of our Christmas parties. To this very day, Grandma Fran is the lasagna-making matriarch of our family. As for myself, I don't feel the need to compete with my mother, her sisters, or anybody else."

Maria fluttered her eyelashes coyly, and said, "Mommy, I enjoy competing. I'm not afraid of it."

I couldn't help but smile when I saw Maria's little horns of pride prop up her dented halo.

I said, "I've never been the competitive type. Doesn't it take a lot of energy to be that way?"

Maria said, "Maybe, if you're afraid of it. Mom, you shouldn't be afraid of competing with anybody. You're an excellent cook. You know how to throw a party better than anybody."

I said, "Thank you for your vote of confidence. It's just that I think people are a lot happier when they try to do their best at whatever they're good at doing, and they do not try to compete with family members and friends. You've got the brains and the beauty. Even if you made up your mind to stop competing, I have a feeling that some of your friends would still regard you as a force to be reckoned with. I want you to know that I will always love you, even when you're not 'the shining star.'"

Maria said, "I love you more, Mommy!"

One day, two of Maria's college friends ended her friendship with her. The loss of friendship came as a shock and saddened Maria. It saddened me too because it was not the kind of college experience I wanted my daughter to have. Based on what Maria told me, it sounded as though she had done her best to be a good friend, but in two girls' eyes, Maria failed miserably. They would not forgive the one thing Maria failed to do, and they did not acknowledge the other things that Maria had done to nurture their relationship. Maria made a handful of other friends while she was in undergraduate school, but she never reconciled with two of the girls that she was originally very close to while she lived in the dorms.

I think it is a tragedy when friendships and relationships come to an end. I regard the severing of a relationship as being a great loss in the game of life and love. Nobody wins when our relationships end. It's a lose-lose situation. We all get upset with friends and family members at times. How we decide to handle our disappointments can make or break any relationship.

Some of the ways that I handle disappointments with my friends and family members is by putting those relationships on the backburner until I cool off or until I forget about the way in which a friend or family member let me down. I believe our relationships can last if we are willing to ride out a storm, and we are willing to give our wounds a chance to heal.

I'm aware of the fact that God places some people in my life to help me accomplish God's plan for my life. Other times, I am aware that I have been placed in somebody's life to help them accomplish God's plan for their life. That is why I avoid ending relationships. If I feel as though I have inadvertently burned a bridge, I will try to put the fire out and rebuild the bridge.

If someone ruffles my feathers, I demote them (in my mind) to a second-class angel until their behavior improves, and they begin operating like a first-class angel. I like to keep in mind that there is always the possibility that a person who is not operating like a first-class angel at this moment, will begin operating like a first-class angel later in the day, the next day, or perhaps someday in the future. Some of the ways that a second-class angel can regain their status as a first-class angel is by performing an act of kindness or doing something that enhances or strengthens our relationship. If there is a rift that needs mending in one of my relationships, I prefer to wait and see if my relationship will be restored and improve over time rather than end a relationship.

I do my best to operate as a first-class angel. However, there are times when someone rubs me the wrong way, and I will operate like a second-class angel. If I catch myself operating that way, I will attempt to do something good to regain my status as a first-class angel. When I demote myself to a second-class angel due to poor behavior, I won't let myself off the hook until I have tried to make amends, or I have done something nice for the first-class angel whose feathers I have ruffled.

When I feel an urgent need to bridge the gap in my relationship with someone who I demoted to a second-class angel, I will extend the first olive branch by doing something nice for them. I try to keep in mind that if I would like someone to act like a first-class angel that I must be a beacon of light that shows them the way. After I have shown them the way by extending an olive branch, I will ask a second-class angel to do something nice to make amends. I might ask a second-class angel for a hug after we have quarreled. I might ask that we go out for lunch or that we watch one of our favorite shows together. Sometimes I select something that I hope will be uplifting for both of us. Other times I will ask the offending party/second-class angle to do something nice for me, and for me only. After the second-class angel has done something nice to make amends and our relationship is restored, they earn back their wings, and they regain their status as a first-class angel.

Joe and I rarely argue, but one day I became angry at Joe right before our annual Auburn/LSU party that we host for Joe's benefit because he is a huge Auburn football fan. I had been away from home before the game for over a week visiting with my children up north. Joe told me before I decided to drive north for Maria's birthday that it would not be a problem, and we would work together to throw the party. Since I was out of town, I was living under the delusion that Joe was going to pitch in for the party more than usual.

While I was away, I talked to Joe. He told me that he had purchased four bags of Doritos, some paper plates, and the paper cups for the party. I have not served Doritos at a party since seventh grade. That's when I started to get a little nervous about the party. I like to make a fuss when I invite people to my house for a party. I usually serve a huge spread with enough food left over for a week.

I said, "Okay. Could you please go out and purchase the ice, beer, and the pop so that when I get home, I won't have to shop for the heavy stuff."

Joe said, "No problem."

I decided to take a different route home because I wanted to spend one night visiting with my cousin Juli and her husband who were staying in the Ozarks. When I arrived at the Four Seasons Hotel in Missouri, I called Joe to let him know that I missed him and that one day he and I needed to visit the Ozarks together. Then I let him know that it would probably take longer to get home than I anticipated because there were mountains in the Ozarks. For all my life, I thought the Ozarks were lakes. I had no idea that there was a beautiful mountain range in the Midwest.

After spending one night at the Four Seasons Hotel, I got back on the road early in the morning. Much to my surprise, there was one mountain range after another for hundreds of miles, with many one-lane winding roads. As I was driving, I kept screaming at the top of my lungs, "God this is insane! I can't believe I am doing this!" It was thrilling and scary in that it was my first time driving by myself through the mountains. My hands were aching from gripping the wheel too tightly.

When I finally reached the flatlands of Arkansas and Louisiana, it started raining. I got home late Friday evening after driving more than thirteen hours. I never stopped at the store to pick up the other items that we needed for the party. When I walked in the door, Joe proudly announced that he had washed all the dishes.

I said, "That's nice, considering that I was not here to dirty the dishes."

Ping. I placed a dent in my halo for sarcasm.

I looked around the kitchen, and most of it was clean. Joe did a good job, but I was too weary to tell him. Ping. I placed another dent in my halo for my sin of neglect.

I looked down and saw dirt and dead grass scattered all over the floors. Disappointment set in. Joe had said that he was going wash the floors before I got home. The main area of the house looked like the dust bunnies had an Easter parade at my house. I glanced at the counter. The paper plates and the plastic cups that Joe purchased did not match and were not our team colors.

I said, "What time are people going to show up tomorrow?"

Joe said, "I told everybody to come at noon."

I said, "What time is the football game?"

Joe said, "It starts at 2:30."

I wanted to say, "You told people to come two and a half hours before the game started when you knew that I was out of town all week? Couldn't you have given me a little more time to prepare?" I didn't say it. I bit my tongue.

I was sorry that I had come back home in time for the Auburn/LSU football game. I wished that I had been the one to leave Joe in a lurch instead of the other way around. At that moment, I demoted Joe from first-class angel to second-class angel.

Joe got up from his Lazy Boy and hugged me. I was too weary to hug him back. I felt like a zombie and went straight to bed. I woke up early Saturday morning and dragged myself out of bed. I made an extra strong cup of coffee and started preparing side dishes for the party with random items I found in the pantry, knowing that there was probably not enough time to go grocery shopping. Then I cleaned up the mess I made while preparing the side dishes. The entire time I kept looking at the clock that kept ticking, trying to figure if there was enough time to run to the grocery store to purchase some Italian sausage to go with the sandwiches from Jimmy John's.

While I was working in the kitchen, Joe slipped out the door into the backyard. I peered out the window and saw that Joe was hosing down the deck and had placed a new corn hole out on the grass that he purchased on Amazon several weeks before. A few minutes later I looked outside again and saw Joe in the pool, slowly and methodically vacuuming it... the pool that I knew nobody at the party would use. Joe came back inside the house. He was still wet.

I said, "Do we have ice, beer, and pop for the coolers?"

Joe said, "Yes, I got it before you woke up."

Joe scored a point in the game of life and love for getting something right.

Less than two hours before the party, Joe announced that he was weary. He sat down on his Lazy Boy, grabbed his clicker, and turned on the pregame show. Joe's decision to kick up his feet and relax during crunch time before a party instantaneously transformed me into a second-class angel.

I said, "You know what? I'm tired too. I think I am going to sit down and relax with you."

Ping. I placed another dent in my halo for being passive-aggressive on purpose. Of course, I could not relax. I felt like Mount Vesuvius getting ready to erupt at any second.

I said, "Joe, I noticed that you put some new games outside on the lawn. Did you pick up the dog poop? If you didn't, people might track dog poop into the house."

Joe said, "It's okay. It doesn't matter if someone tracks dog poop into the house."

I couldn't believe my ears. I was thinking, *Who are you, and where is my husband when I need him the most?*

I said, "You're okay with people tracking dog poop into our house?"

Joe said, "The dog gets poop on his paws all the time, and he tracks it into the house."

I said, "That's not true! I watch him when he poops. He always steps around it. He tracks grass back into our house as do we, but not his poop!"

Joe said, "Relax! It rained a lot last night. I found one soft dog poop out there and washed it into the grass with the hose."

I said, "You didn't check good enough! There's more than one dog poop out there!"

Then I jumped up from my chair, picked up the pair of shoes that Joe had left by the TV and the shoes which Tony left on foyer floor, and I threw them, one by one, a hundred miles an hour into the bedrooms located off our TV room.

The pair of shoes that landed in Tony's bedroom startled him and woke him up.

Tony shouted, "Mom, what's the matter? Why are you throwing shoes?"

I yelled, "That's what Italian women do when we are angry!"

Then I got out the vacuum and started furiously vacuuming so Joe couldn't watch the pregame show. Joe got up from his Lazy Boy and vanished into the bedroom. After I was finished vacuuming, Tony walked up to me and said sympathetically, "Mom, is there anything I can do to help you get ready for the party?"

I said, "Yes, that would be nice. The first thing we must do is check the backyard for dog poop."

Tony and I went into the backyard to do a dog poop inspection, and no dog poop was found!

I said, "God is good. He washed away most of the poop with the rain except for one."

Tony said, "Mom, everything is going to be okay. Our house looks cleaner than most people's."

I said, "You always tell me that before a party. I don't like acting this way. I'm just upset that Joe decided to tell everybody to show up at noon. He knew ahead of time that I was operating on a tight schedule. He should have told people to show up a half hour before the football game, not two and a half hours before the game.

"Joe knows how to manage an oil refinery, and everything there is to know about the laws of physics, but he does not realize how much energy is required to throw a party. I am running low on energy right now.

"Just like a typical guy, Joe spent the morning cleaning outside. Men do that before parties because they realize that the outside of the house is a reflection on them, and the inside of the house is a reflection on the woman.

"In Joe's mind, he has played his part to get things ready for the party, and he expects me to play my part. It's how the game is played. I have no choice but to play by the rules.

"Joe is probably in the house, taking a nice long shower right now. Then he is going to drive to Jimmy Johns to pick up some sandwiches. I have an hour and a half to get this house in order before people start walking through the door. I don't think there will be enough time to make this house and myself look presentable! I have never been so unprepared for a party in my life."

Tony said, "Call Jimmy John's and tell them to deliver the sandwiches. That way Joe can stay here and help you."

I said, "It will be better if he leaves the house so that I can cool off."

Tony came to the rescue as a first-class angel. He allowed me to vent my heart, and he did everything that I asked him to do. He mopped the floors, cleaned the window panes on the entry door, dusted the top of the mantel above the fireplace, and the shelves I could not reach. The finishing touch was that Tony hung some decorations on the wall. While Tony was busy, I checked off all the items on my checklist and was able to breathe easier. Tony was my hero who saved the day!

Halo Hint

Helping a woman get the interior of her home ready for a party during crunch time is a remarkable quality of a first-class angel, especially a young one!

Joe tried to do some damage control when he got home by offering to cut up the sandwiches into fourths. He asked me for a tray, knowing that even though we were serving sandwiches as the main course that "presentation is everything." Although cutting up the sandwiches and arranging them nicely on a party tray was considerate on Joe's part, it was not enough for him to earn back his wings. He was still a second-class angel in my eyes. Sadly, so was I.

I went into the master bathroom to take a quick shower and freshen up. It wasn't long before the door-bell rang, and the first guest arrived. Ready or not, it was show time. I didn't look my best, but my appearance had to suffice. All I could do was try to get my inner beauty to shine through, even though I still hadn't earned back my wings or my status as a first-class angel.

During the party, Joe sat on his Lazy Boy and finished watching pregame shows, and more than one college football game with his co-workers. After several guests arrived and settled in, I went up to Joe and rubbed out the tension in his shoulders as a way of letting him know that I was no longer angry. My loving gesture directed at Joe was my way of extending an olive branch to mend the rift in our relationship. My public display of affection was also intended to heal the pain which I caused Joe earlier that day when I flipped out. Rubbing Joe's shoulders also enabled me to earn back my wings, regain my status as a first-class angel, and feel good about myself.

A few minutes later, I sat in a chair that I pulled up next to Joe. Then I swung my legs on top of his lap and said, "My feet are tired and achy. Would you rub them for me?"

Joe asked, "You want me to rub your feet?" as if to say, "Is this the time or the place for this kind of thing?"

I smiled and said sweetly, "Yes, I would like you to rub my feet."

Joe rubbed my feet, just the way I like them rubbed for one minute. Then I lifted my legs off Joe's lap and walked away. The one-minute foot massage served more than one purpose. It released the tension from my body, and it healed my pain which Joe caused by not manning-up as much as he could have to help with the party. Joe earned back his wings and regained his status as a first-class angel by his willingness to rub my feet even though it was only for one minute! The rift that was caused by both of us was fully mended!

Here is a review of the three basic steps to mend the rift in a relationship:

1) Be the first person to extend an olive branch by doing something nice for the person no matter who was at fault for causing the rift.

   o If you were at fault, this is your way of saying, "I'm sorry" without the use of words.

   o If the other person was at fault, this is your way of saying, "I am ready to forgive you" without the use of words.

2) After the person has accepted the olive branch, give them some time to experience inner healing and a feeling of restored love, joy, and peace.

3) When the time feels right, ask the person to do something nice **for you** or **with you** so you can experience inner healing and a feeling of restored love, joy, and peace.

If a person is reasonable and the relationship is a healthy one, we can expect that a person will graciously accept an olive branch and will play their part to mend the rift by extending an olive branch in return, especially when they are prompted to do so. This method goes a long way in mending the rift in my relationships. If you decide to utilize this method, I hope and pray that it will do the same for yours.

You already have some proof that my method for mending a rift can turn wrongs into a right, and a second-class angel into a first-class angel. However, no method for mending rifts is foolproof. There is no cookie-cutter way to heal our wounds or our relationships. A lot of times, we must live and learn by trial and error.

When trying to mend a rift in our relationships, we must try to remember what Mr. Rogers and the Bible tells us, "There are many ways to say, 'I love you,'" and love covers a multitude of sins. (1 Peter 4:8)

Forgiveness

If a person is humble enough to admit to making a mistake, even in part, it's best to forgive them and hope for a better tomorrow. As first-class angels, we must try to remember "the seventy times seven rule of forgiveness" that Jesus talked about in Matthew 18:22. What Jesus meant when He said that we must forgive not just seven times, but seventy times seven times is that it is best to extend forgiveness as often as necessary. There isn't a fixed number, per se, in that we should not keep a record of wrongs. (1 Corinthians 13:5) Forgiveness is the biblical secret to maintaining life-long relationships.

Looking at people through the eyes of love and compassion, seeing the best in people, and minimizing their shortcomings is essential to maintaining life-long relationships.

Halo Hints

When we forgive a person, it heals our relationship. When we look for the best in a person, it helps us to realize what is right about our relationship.

If you look for the best in people, you already possess one of the essential qualities of a first-class angel. You wouldn't have picked up this book if you didn't already have what it takes to be a first-class angel! I hope this book shows you what you're doing right, but it also provides you with some great stories and halo-hints to improve your relationships so that you can fly to a higher realm of love.

On that note, let's take a little music break to listen to Alabama sing, "Angels Among Us." As we listen to this song, let's pray that God will give us the ability to be "a first-class angel."

CHAPTER 7

Little Things that Make Life Easier & Breezier

Before I moved to Louisiana, I experienced many high notes with my children. We also had our fair share of low notes after their father and I went through a divorce. I did my best to ensure that all my children were involved in activities that would take their mind off their parents' divorce whether it was setting up play dates for my younger children, sending my daughter off on a mission trip, or ensuring that all five of my children were having fun in sports or other activities.

My children were between the ages of three and fourteen when their father and I split up. Having lost my dreams of having a marriage that would last a lifetime, I had no desire to see my family fragment into smaller pieces. The threat seemed real every time one of my sons told me that he wanted to live with his dad. I knew my sons missed living with their father, but I also knew their desire to live with him often surfaced when they were resisting my instruction. It was during those times when I looked up to heaven and said, "God, why did you give me so many sons?"

My sister-in-law, Sue, also a mother of four sons, told me many years ago that boys respond best to a commanding voice. I operated at a deficit because I do not possess a commanding voice. I have a childlike voice. I also do not possess the kind of look that tells a child that a mother means business. To make matters worse, when my children are naughty, I cannot keep a straight face. I have always found the naughty things that they do to be amusing. I have raised five first-class angels that have many dents in their halos.

The outburst that I described in an earlier chapter when I threw the shoes one hundred miles an hour is not the way I usually operate. Although I do erupt now and then, I am like a volcano that remains inactive for long periods of time.

Signage Is Important

I took a business class a long time ago, and I learned that signage is important. I am the kind of woman who places signs in the house, hoping that people living in my house will read the signs and follow the rules. For example, for many years I had not just one but two signs with the Ten Commandments hanging on the walls of my house, one for the adults, and one for the children. The Ten Commandments come in handy, especially for those of us who are married. Hopefully, we will not bear false witness or commit adultery, and we will serve as a good example to our children.

I didn't hang up the two signs with the Ten Commandments when I moved to the South. Since Jesus explained in words and in parables that the greatest commandment is love, I decided to replace the Ten Commandments with a sign in my house that says, "Do all things with Love."

I have two signs with "The House Rules." One House Rules sign is in the foyer. The other is in my kitchen. The House Rules are spelled out for everybody. If any of my family members (including me) needs "a sign" that we're supposed to act like first-class angels, there are signs everywhere in my home. There are at least two or three spiritual or inspirational signs in almost every room that explain to people how to win at life and love.

Halo Hint

If a mother has enough signs in her home that contain words of wisdom, her home becomes a book of wisdom!

It's a Family Affair

Because I do not come across as authoritative, I had always felt the need to rely on a more authoritative person who is good about living by the rules to help me enforce the rules when my children, mainly my sons, got out of hand or were causing a ruckus. After I went through a divorce, I relied heavily on my mother, father, brothers, and my two sisters-in-law to help me raise my children until I married Joe.

I realize that parents are supposed to be the primary educators of their children. However, it is also important to select our special team of first-class angels to teach our children how to win at life and love. Most people don't have to look very far in that we can find first-class angels within our own families. I relied on the first-class angels within my family because I never thought for one moment that I was the heroic, fearless kind of woman who could pull off raising my five children by myself.

When I read life stories about famous people, they always talk about not only how their parents influenced them, but also how other relatives impacted their lives. Reese Witherspoon has written a beautiful book called, *Whiskey in a Teacup*, that tells stories about how she learned to be a strong woman while retaining her femininity from her mother and her grandmother. As I read the book, I was impressed by the vast amount of knowledge and life skills Reese Witherspoon picked up simply by spending time with her family.

I loved when Reese told us that her grandmother said, "it was a combination of beauty and strength that made southern women 'whiskey in teacups.'" It is amazing how a grandmother's words of wisdom can shape a person's character. I also found it endearing when Reese said that her mother had a great laugh, and her laugh egged Reese on to become an actress.

If a mother's laugh could inspire a child to go into show business and a grandmother's words can shape a person's character, imagine the impact several adult family members can have on a child when they spend quality time with them.

Reese also talked about inviting family to stay under one roof, such as her brother, who loves fixing her car and serves as her handyman without being asked. She said that her son enjoys following her brother around, trying to gain wisdom.

After my ex-husband and I separated and divorced, my father who was fighting cancer, came to my house to teach my two older sons how to drive the John Deere and mow the lawn. Every week, no matter how hot it was outside or how horrible my dad felt, he showed up to supervise my sons as they mowed the lawn. Before my dad left my house, he always reminded them to respect and obey their mom. I could write another book about all the things my dad did to have a positive impact on the lives of his children, grandchildren, nieces, and nephews. As a token of my love and appreciation, all I will say is that my father was a first-class angel and winner at the game of life and love.

When my two older sons were in their teens and started giving me too much attitude, all I had to do was call my brother Ray. Ray would take them on long bike rides on Saturday afternoons to help them burn off steam. Then he would talk to them and remind them how important it is to love and respect their mom. The love and support Ray directed at us makes him a first-class angel and winner at the game of life and love.

Sometimes I would tell my brother Lou and sister-in-law Sue about the problems I was having with my children, and they would spend time talking some sense into them. It embarrassed them when I snitched on them to other family members. However, my children needed to have a consequence. A bit of embarrassment served as their consequence. Lou and Sue's willingness to help me teach my children right from wrong makes them first-class angels and winners at the game of life and love.

Halo Hint

Mentoring and teaching children how to win at life and love are important aspects of a first-class angel's job description.

Children grow up having more of an advantage if several members of a family work together to mentor children and show them how to win at life and love. That's why it is so extremely important to get along with all our family members. If there is a rift, we must go out of our way to mend the rift. If we burn a bridge, we must put out the fire and do our best to rebuild the bridge. That way our family members remain our closest allies, and they do not turn into our enemies or acquaintances that we knew once upon a time.

When families do not live close together, we must go out of our way to spend much needed time together. Although it takes extra time, energy, and resources to see family members who live far away, it is that much more meaningful every time we get together.

Southern Respect

I could not help but notice when I moved to the South, that children are trained to say, "Yes Ma'am" to their mother and their female superiors the same way that those who serve in the military are required to say, "Yes, Sir," to their superiors every time they are addressed. I wasn't accustomed to it. At first, it made me feel twenty years older every time a southern child said, "Yes, Ma'am" at the end of my sentences. It took three or four years to get used to hearing "Yes Ma'am." Now, its music to my ears!

When a child says, "Yes Ma'am" to their mother or another female superior in the South, not only does the child affirm what their mother or female superior is saying to them, but the child is also required to do what they are told to do. If the child does not say, "Yes, Ma'am," and do what they are supposed to do, their mothers provide swift consequences.

Halo Hint

Teaching a child to say, "Yes, Ma'am" and "Yes, Sir" as a sign of respect to their mother, their father, a teacher, or an authority figure is a great habit to form in children from the time they are little love bugs!

I do not lump my daughter in with my four sons because Maria was in a class by herself. I truly thank God that He gave me a first-born daughter because she was a first-class angel that helped me raise her four brothers. Maria was an excellent little mommy. She was good at getting her brothers to toe the line. The words, "Yes, Ma'am" were hardly ever used in our household, but the words, "Yes, Maria" were used all the time!

I love that Reese Witherspoon's book, *Whiskey in a Teacup* is like a training manual for every woman to become a Southern lady or more ladylike in general. The Southern way is to American women what the Parisian way is to European women.

One thing I would like to change regarding "proper etiquette" is that if I invite someone to my house, instead of receiving a thank-you note, I would like to receive an invitation to their house. Reciprocation is the Yankee way of saying thank-you. Inviting someone into our homes is like inviting someone into our hearts. Anytime a person reciprocates, it solidifies our relationship and makes it feel much more genuine.

Parents Must Pray Everyday

We live in a world where we have witnessed many school shootings. Sex trafficking has become a major threat to young people and even infants. Raising children in the 1990s and the turn of the century was hard enough, but it keeps getting harder. There is a lot of good in the world, but there is also a lot of evil. I feel such an urgent need to tell young parents to pray for the protection of your children and cover every aspect of their lives with prayer.

My go-to-book was and still is *The Power of a Praying Mom* by Stormie Omartian. When my children got older, I also purchased Stormie's book called, *The Power of Praying for Adult Children.* I also have other go-to-prayers such as the Rosary, The Chaplet of Divine Mercy, and The Stations of the Cross. God called me to pray in the Spirit. He kept calling me for thirty years until I accepted the Holy Spirit's gift of prayer.

Not only do we need extra guardian angels watching over our families at every moment, but my rationale is also that if I cannot get my children to do what I would like them to do, that the Lord will have to intervene to get them to do what He wants them to do. It does not mean that I do not try to get my children to do what they are supposed to do. However, if I can't get them to do what they are supposed to do, the ultimate responsibility rests on God's shoulders. My job is to pray for my children until they arrive one day in heaven. If we gain the whole world and do not make our journey to heaven, we've lost the game of life and love.

My personality is like that of Mary who sat at the feet of Jesus more than, Martha, who went above and beyond the call of duty to serve others as depicted in the Bible. When I read the story about Martha and Mary, I get the impression that Mary had a Type B personality and Martha had a Type A.

My observations of people who possess Type B personalities is that they do not want to stress out about things. They operate at their best when they pace themselves, and there is balance in their lives. Type B personalities have a difficult time working at a fast pace unless the winds of inspiration brush against their wings or there is an urgent need to meet a deadline. They want to live, laugh, love, and have cozy, comfortable lives.

My impression of Type A personalities is that they are perfectionists, and they have a great need to be highly productive. They put pressure on themselves and apply pressure to the people around them to have a good, preferably an outstanding, work ethic. Type A personalities want to be admired for their hard work, determination, and accomplishments.

I hate the feeling of being stressed out, especially in my own home. Unless I have a good reason to stretch myself beyond my comfort zone, I don't place a lot of pressure on myself. Preparing for a party is a different story. I want everybody in my household to shift into a higher gear when we are preparing for a party until the first guest walks through the door. However, the purpose of having a party is to live it up for a little while, laugh, love one another, and connect with at least one person on a deeper level.

Parenting Tips from a Type B Mom

It is important for parents to know that there is good noise and bad noise. The sound of children playing is good noise unless it is past their bedtime or past the point where mom, dad, grandma, or grandpa can't take it anymore.

Listening to a parent yelling at their children to clean up their messes is bad noise. Yelling causes stress. It also causes too much cortisol to be released into the body, causing belly fat. People do not operate at their best when they are under stress, especially children. I want to remind mothers that making a stern or angry face also causes us to get wrinkles. If we are going to have wrinkles, we want them to be smile lines.

Raising our voice should be reserved for something of great importance. Raising our voice all the time is no different than crying wolf; sooner or later children will learn to tune a parent out. Raising our voice occasionally has more shock appeal.

One way to avoid losing our cool is to get every child in the household to serve a little. Some children are naturally more generous than others. Some children are stingy and resent when we ask them to do anything.

I have never placed big demands on my children. At times I asked for "some help and cooperation." If a mom or a dad asks a child to do one small task most will do it, even a child who tries to buck the system. Over a period of several years, a parent can gradually stretch a child's generosity to **pitch in** and **give more of themselves**. Generous acts of self-giving love will come naturally to a child when a parent applies gentle pressure on his or her children on a consistent basis, over time.

If you want to see how gently applied pressure works, watch the movie, *Shawshank Redemption*. In that movie, an innocent man was unjustly sent to prison for the murder of his wife. He managed to break through a thick wall of solid rock utilizing a small chisel. It took him several years to slowly chisel his way through the rock wall, but he finally managed to escape from the highly secured prison.

Shawshank Redemption is symbolic to us in that it demonstrates that we don't have to operate as a bulldozer or a sledgehammer to have a breakthrough with our children. Sixteen or eighteen years of gently applied pressure is just enough time for us to get our children to provide loving service to others, or at least, to take care of themselves. If it takes more than sixteen or eighteen years, we can keep applying gentle pressure for as long as we live. Sooner or later, with the help of God's grace, we should be able to get through a stubborn child's thick skull.

I did not enjoy having assigned chores as a child. So, I never assigned chores to my children. Their father, my father, and Joe assigned chores to them. Joe and my dad used cash to get them to do outdoor chores, and their father always promised to do something fun with them after they were done doing their chores. In other words, they used bribery to get my kids to do what they wanted them to do. There's nothing wrong with bribing children to do what they ought to do. I am not complaining. I am happy that, my first-class angels in training have some first-class angels in their lives who resort to bribery.

My primary goal as a mother has been for my children to perform a specific task when I ask them to do it. The sooner they do it, the better. I want them to do things for me to make me happy--the same way that I do things for them to make them happy when they ask me to do things for them.

It makes me even happier when my children do things to make me happy of their own volition without being asked. Like for example, when my son Johnny brings home flowers from Brookshire that he found on sale, for no other reason than to show me that he loves me.

I recall a time when I woke up with three feet of snow that drifted into my driveway. I called my children and said, "Looks like there will not be any school today, we're snowed in. It's a blizzard out there! I have never seen this much snow in our driveway. It might be a while before I can get to the grocery store. It's heavy snow; it must weigh a ton!"

Without being asked, my children got dressed in warm clothes and went outside to shovel my driveway. They got three feet of snow shoveled in less than ten minutes.

I went outside and said, "Holy Smokes! You kids are amazing! I thought we were going to be snowed in for days! Run over to Miss Linda's house to shovel them out of their driveway. Even if Mr. Z offers, do not take any money!"

My children were gone for most of the morning. They took it upon themselves to shovel many driveways. They came home, very excited.

One said, "Mom, we can't believe it! Some man paid us a hundred dollars to shovel his driveway!"

I said, "You should not have taken that much money for one driveway!"

One said, "We told him it was too much money. The man insisted and said that we were worth it!"

Do you want to know why it important to me that my children do things because I asked, or they do things without being asked? Simply because one day they will probably get married, and their spouse will ask them to do things. If they can do what their spouse asks them to do with love and joy in their heart, it will make their spouse happy. If they do sweet things for their spouse without being asked, it will make their spouse even happier.

Halo Hint

Doing things when asked and not asked are important aspects of a first-class angel's job description.

The Messy Bedroom Dilemma

I allowed my children to have messy bedrooms and closets because it was easier to close the door than clean a bedroom or a closet during the busyness of our daily lives.

I have noticed that if a child wants or needs more organization in their personal space, they will clean and organize it without being asked. Of course, the children who don't feel the need to be neat and organized, won't do anything without a little nudge.

I cannot take any credit for my approach to bedroom maintenance. I learned it from my mother. My mother loves things to be neat and organized. Her bedroom was always in perfect order, but she closed the doors of her children's messy bedrooms and looked the other way. Every so often she told us to clean our bedroom, but not often. I truly appreciated my mother's laze fare approach to bedroom maintenance when I was a child in that it created less stress and more peace in our household. For that reason, I followed in my mother's footsteps.

Now and then I walk into my children's bedrooms, and I say, "This room is getting to be a little too messy. It's time to clean it up." They usually clean it up within a day or two.

There has been more than one time when I had four sons sharing the same bedroom. It was rare that I ever blew the whistle on their messy bedroom. It seemed like a hopeless cause. A funny thing happened. Every so often, my sons took it upon themselves to rearrange their furniture and clean their bedroom without being asked. I guess they had reached a point where they couldn't handle their clutter or their mess.

I was always so proud of them whenever they took the initiative. I would say, "You guys did a great job! What you did to this bedroom is amazing!"

Admittedly, there are better ways to manage bedrooms and closets other than leaving children to their own devices. If you have a better idea, implement it. Some women have a flair for arranging storage nooks when they do not have enough drawer space or closet space. Some women have garage sales twice a year to rid their house of clutter.

Whatever you do, teach your children "your way" in a peaceful, loving way. As I said in the first chapter, "first-class angels strive to be at peace with themselves and others." It is important to model that behavior to first-class angels in training.

I look at messes this way: people pay extra money to purchase jeans that are worn out and have holes in them. If it is perfectly acceptable for people to look messy when they go out in public, then it is perfectly acceptable for certain rooms in my house to be messy in private. We need to feel comfortable in our homes, the same way that we are comfortable in our favorite pair of blue jeans. If we keep odors away, and mildew at bay, our shabby-chic lifestyle is perfectly okay!

Joe's way of dealing with our shabby-chic lifestyle is to have separate bathroom vanities for each person. Each person has their own workspace in their bedroom or another section of our house. Joe's private workspace is upstairs in his man cave. Tony and Johnny, each has a workspace in their bedroom. As for myself, I have a floating workspace so that I can have a change of atmosphere when I am writing.

When it is all said and done, Joe wants everybody in our household to have separate messes. Keeping messes separated makes our lives easier and breezier. If anybody needs to find something, we can find it in our own mess.

Picking My Battles

Just like my mother, I can be a real stickler when I need to be. Food is not allowed in the bedrooms. If my children break this rule, I tell them that we could get bedbugs. Most children do not want bedbugs and will comply. However, I check every so often to ensure that they are complying. If I find food or a sugary substance in the bedroom, I shout at them and remind them that we do not want any bedbugs. I do not enjoy raising my voice, but this is an exception.

I also place trash bins in our bedrooms and the bathrooms with the hope that the trash will land inside the bins. Trash bins prevent rooms from becoming too trashy. There is a fine line between shabby-chic and trashy.

If I walk into a bedroom or a bathroom, and one of the trash bins is getting full or overflowing, I empty it. Not making a big deal over filled-up trash bins and serving as the trash picker-upper is my way of saying "I love you," and not sweating the small stuff, something I learned from Richard Carlson, Ph.D., the author of *Don't Sweat the Small Stuff... and it's all small stuff—simple ways to keep the little things from taking over your life.*

Joe's Stress-Free Approach to Laundry

After Joe and I got married, he suggested that we purchase one hamper for each person in the house and wash each person's clothes separately. He explained that it would save time because we wouldn't have to sort everybody's laundry when it came out of the dryer. After a while, Joe got tired of waiting for me to do his laundry, and he started doing his own laundry. My two younger son followed Joe's lead, and they started doing their laundry, sometime in their teens. I never asked Joe to do his laundry. Nor did I ask my two younger sons to do their laundry. I simply forgot to do their laundry, and they took it upon themselves to pick up the slack. I love when my family members do things without being asked.

However, I always fold their clothes after they come out of the dryer because several years ago a first-class angel named, "Miss Linda" taught me how to fold clothes with love. I put Joe's clothes away for him, but I place my sons' folded clothes on their beds and tell them to put them away. I want to think that they do it because I lovingly tell them to do it, but it might be that they appreciate that I lightened their workload.

I also tell the guys that if they want their laundry washed that they should tell me, and to place their laundry bins where I can see them—in the hallway just outside the laundry room. I don't mind doing laundry, but I need occasional reminders. Joe, Johnny, and Tony have learned to go with the flow and deal with my idiosyncrasies.

Halo Hint

The ability to make light of someone's short-comings is a wonderful quality of a first-class angel.

Long before I married Joe, I warned him that if he was looking for a housekeeping goddess that I was not the woman. Joe said, "That's okay, as long as you're willing to work together." When I drop the ball, Joe picks it up. Joe and I are alike in that, most of the time, we do not sweat the small stuff.

Halo Hint

Picking up the ball when somebody drops it and not sweating the small stuff are awesome qualities of a first-class angel.

When adults **do not sweat the small stuff and take the initiative to do the small stuff with love in their hearts,** children are more loving, cooperative, and willing to "pitch in" and work as a team. We might not operate like a finely oiled machine, but it does not matter. I'd rather be peaceful, loving, and strive to keep things light and breezy.

On that note, let's take a little music break to listen to Cat Stevens sing, "Peace Train." As we listen to it, let us remember that peace starts first in our hearts and then in our homes.

CHAPTER 8

God Sent a Fleet of First-Class Angels

When I was a child, my mother gave me chores to do on Saturday. I learned right away that it was not any fun doing chores. I would rather sing and dance in my parents' living room than do my chores. I would rather do anything than do my chores. My mother allowed me to sing and dance for as long as I wanted with the proviso that I got all my chores done before I went out to play. An hour's worth of chores took five or six hours because I felt the need to turn every Saturday into a big musical production.

How Do You Solve a Problem Like Francesca?

When I was a young mother, God sent me a first-class angel. Her name was Maria. Maria usually did what she was supposed to do when I asked her to do it. Maria was also a spitfire. She often got her brothers to do what they were supposed to do when they were supposed to do it. One day when her father came home, after a long day at work, he observed our routine and said, "Who is the mother around here? You or Maria?"

I said, "Maria and I are doing a great job raising these boys together. Where have you been lately?"

God also sent me another first-class angel. Her name was Molly, and she was a character on a children's TV show. Molly taught my children and me how to do "the ten-minute tidy." When a main room of the house became too messy, I turned on the timer, and we cleaned as fast as we could for five or ten minutes. Anybody can muster up the determination to clean for five or ten minutes, even me!

The ten-minute tidy is my favorite cleaning tip for mothers with young children. Children are more willing to clean up when mom or dad is cleaning right beside them, doing a five- or ten-minute tidy.

To this day, I still set the timer for ten minutes when I don't feel like cleaning. Even when I don't rush, I can cover a lot of territory in ten minutes.

God sent me not just one, but some other first-class angels to help pick up the slack. After I had my third child, my mother used to come over without being asked and helped me with the laundry once a week.

God also sent a first-class angel named Chloe when I was experiencing post-partum depression with my third child. Chloe, my young neighbor, showed up unannounced at my doorstep and introduced herself to me.

Little Chloe happened to show up the day before Charley's baptism and asked if I needed a babysitter. Right before Chloe showed up, I had told the Lord that I did not know how I was going to throw a party the following day because I had nothing prepared. I loved babies, but I was sleep deprived and felt like I had bitten off more than I could chew having three children close in age.

I didn't want to take three children under the age of five to the grocery store. After running out of hands, I was genuinely afraid that I would lose one of my children. Not only did Chloe babysit my children while I went to the store, but she also helped tidy up the house! She gladly did it, without being asked, with love and joy in her heart!

Little Chloe was my children's babysitter for about five years. She always tidied things up every time I went to the grocery store. She'd straighten out my counters in the kitchen and get my children to pick up their toys. That's when I got in the habit of grocery shopping just about every day. Even if it was for only for a half-hour or forty-five minutes, it was a much-needed mommy break.

I have a feeling that Chloe wanted to come over to play house with my children, and she took just enough stress off my shoulders to make my job as a mother much more enjoyable.

Chloe also babysat for two of my other neighbors. However, I feel blessed to say that Chloe offered to babysit for me before she offered her services to the other neighbors. She showed up in my life, right when I needed her the most.

I must give a special shout out to my sister-in-law, Sue. Sue was the first-class angel that assisted with my first-home birth and almost ended up delivering my baby even though she is a cardiac nurse. While I was suffering from post-partum depression after my third birth, Sue opened her heart and home to my children and me. There were several months when I was so depressed that I could barely take care of my children. Every time I came over, Sue offered to make my children lunch or dinner. I was so depressed that I was useless to everybody. My post-partum depression lasted from late January until spring brought forth sunshine and my depression subsided. I am grateful to God that He gave me an extremely compassionate and loving sister-in-law.

Halo Hint

Mentoring a young mother and assisting her on an emotional level are wonderful undertakings of a first-class angel.

When Chloe became a cheerleader, she told our two neighbors and me that she could no longer babysit. I thought *Oh Dear God, what am I going to do without Chloe?* God is good. He heard my thoughts! A little while later, I met a very nice Christian woman who needed a part-time job. She told me that she had an eighteen-year-old daughter and played a role in raising some of her nieces and nephews. I hired her on the spot as a part-time nanny. Miss Linda showed up in my life three months after I had given birth to my fifth child and shortly after my children's father and I opened a fitness center. I wouldn't have been able to get into shape or attempt to play the part of a co-owner of a fitness center had it not been for Miss Linda.

Moreover, Miss Linda loved talking to my children about Jesus and sharing stories from the Bible. Hiring Miss Linda was like putting a missionary on the payroll to evangelize my children! I regarded it as being the most important aspect of her job description.

Halo Hint

Assisting a mother with young children and helping her to teach them about the love of Jesus are extraordinary undertakings of a first-class angel.

I never asked God to send any of above-mentioned first-class angels to assist me on my mission as a mother. All I can tell you is that I was and still am in the habit of praying in the morning and intermittently throughout the day. When life becomes a challenge, I usually spend more time praying. I can only guess that God must have looked down from heaven and realized that I needed all the help I could get maintaining my home and taking care of my five first-class angels in training. Other than being generous with my fertility and praying, I did not do anything to deserve the assistance of the first-class angels who assisted me when I needed them the most!

Halo Hint

If any person takes the time to pray, God will send first-class angels in human form to assist them along the way!

A Great Parenting Book

I recently found a book called *The One Minute Mother* in a second-hand bookstore. I wish I had discovered this gem a long time ago. The book was written by Spencer Johnson, M.D. and was originally published in the early 1980s. I didn't begin my journey as a mother until 1991, which might explain why I never heard about *The One Minute Mother* while my children were growing up.

The book is only about a hundred pages long, and it shows a mother how to blend an authoritarian approach with a positive approach to parenting to bring out the best in her children. The book shows a mother how to praise her child, help her child set goals by having weekly meetings, and reprimand her child in as little as one minute. There is also a book that accompanies *The One Minute Mother* called *The One Minute Father* by the same author.

Through the years I have come to believe that it is important for people of all ages to set goals for themselves. There is one line from *The One Minute Mother* that can serve as a great halo hint for first-class angels:

"A goal is a dream with a deadline attached to it."

It is important for us to encourage our children to have dreams and goals with deadlines. *The One Minute Mother* shows mothers how to help a child set and reach their goals.

Parents are always trying to instill self-confidence in their children. However, when a child sees that their parent is self-assured, a parent has more authority with their children.

There have been times when my confidence levels were high, and there were times when they were low. It was much easier for me to raise my children when my confidence levels were high. *The One Minute Mother* and *The One Minute Father* each provide pointers that will help parents to keep their confidence levels up even when things are not going right in their personal or professional lives.

I would like to see more parents possess quiet, calm, self-assurance, and savvy while raising their children so that parents can enjoy every minute of being parents because as they say, "the years fly by faster than the blink of an eye."

In addition to writing books, I enjoy giving out books written by my favorite authors as gifts to people. One of my goals is to give *The One Minute Mother* and *The One Minute Father* as gifts to new mothers and fathers in my family and circle of friends. I highly recommend Dr. Spencer Johnson's two books to all moms and dads. His two books should be classified as family classics.

Instilling Responsibility in Teenagers

An easy way to get a sixteen-year-old to operate as a pre-adult is to tell the teenager that he or she must get a job to pay for their car insurance, gas, and entertainment. Having the privilege of driving a car to go out on dates and do fun things (within reason) is a great goal for sixteen-year-olds through eighteen-year-olds to be used as an incentive to help children obtain a job and begin managing some of their own money.

If a child lacks maturity or isn't a good driver, a parent can postpone their child's driving privileges until a parent believes their child is ready to get their license and take on the responsibility of a job.

My son Johnny is now a freshman at a college located only an hour and a half away from home. We've set a goal to get him to come home on weekends once a month. My son Tony is a junior in high school. Tony currently drives himself to school and, also has a part-time job. I'm getting closer to being "an empty nester, with my two youngest sons flying in and out of the nest.

It seems like it was only yesterday that all my children were living in my nest. For now, I am going to write about home life with my children in the present tense. The topics that I will discuss in the remainder of this chapter rang true for all my children.

Celebrations

I place more demands on my children, Joe, and myself when I am getting ready for a party. Before, during, and shortly after parties I am mysteriously transformed from Mary into Martha. My children know that I want to make a good impression on our guests, and they are usually more than willing to work with me to get the house ready for a party.

My children also know that it is my style to indulge our guests with a spread of our family's favorite, festive foods. I often serve a buffet of homemade Italian food mixed with items that are store bought. Knowing that we are going to open our home and share our favorite, festive foods with our guests motivates my children to go above and beyond the call of duty to get our house looking its best. I throw parties or have small gatherings about every four to eight weeks.

I also make special requests on my birthday, during the holidays, and Mother's Day. Instead of asking my children for gifts, I ask them to do things for me. Some of my children are good at organizing things, and I ask them to organize one of the closets or the pantry. At times I ask them to take pictures with me or help fill a large picture frame with photos of our family.

Getting Children to Eat Out of Your Hand

Meal preparation is an ideal time to ask one's son or daughter to take the garbage out, empty the dishwasher, set the table, or serve as a sous chef. When children sense love in the kitchen, they will work with a parent or a grandparent, especially if you make your request known to them using a sweet tone of voice.

When I am cooking with love, I could easily get my children to do favors for me. I've learned that **the best time** to ask children to do something for me is when something is simmering on the stove or baking in the oven. Timing is everything. The anticipation of a good meal causes children to be ten times more cooperative. Even if they say that they do not want to do something because they are watching their favorite TV show, or they are playing a video-game, it is easy to get them to promise to do something for me a while later. After they've made a promise, it is easy to get them to keep their promise. I've noticed that the older my children get, the more cooperative they get.

I can testify that I received many hugs and kisses, and have heard my children say, "I love you, Mom" and my husband says, "I love you honey," many times when I was cooking with love in the kitchen.

To cook with love, you must anticipate the joy the meal will bring to your family while you are cooking. If you allow yourself to get overwhelmed by the amount of work it takes to prepare a meal or you allow the ensuing mess in your kitchen to upset you, the food will not taste good because everybody's moods will sour by the time you sit down to eat the meal.

Halo Hint

Cooking with love helps us to win hearts.

Believe me when I tell you that the proof is in the pudding. My four sons find skinny women unattractive. They prefer a woman who is squeezable and soft, which speaks volumes considering that their father owns a health club. My sons have had opportunities to check out lean, fit women from the time they were young boys, but would gladly pass them up for a cushier woman that cooks for them with love!

One of our favorite dinners is Italian meatloaf and mashed potatoes made with an ample amount of butter and sour cream. Our special occasion dish is Shrimp Francesca, a shrimp and artichoke dish made with Italian bread crumbs. Our other special occasion dish is baked Rigatoni made with the same ingredients as lasagna. My baked rigatoni looks like lasagna jambalaya before I place it in the oven. After it bakes for about fifteen minutes, the cheeses meld the rigatoni together.

One of our favorite family snacks is popcorn, popped the old-fashioned way in a pot on top of the stove. While I am popping the popcorn, my children melt the butter.

My children also love chocolate chip cookies. Giving them a homemade chocolate chip cookie as a reward for good behavior when they were younger was like rewarding them with a gold medal!

I often keep ice-cream in my house, along with a bottle of chocolate syrup and two cans of whipped cream, one for my children, and one unopened can for my guests. My sons have developed a habit of going into the refrigerator and squirting the whipped cream directly into their mouths in between meals to hold them over when they claim that they are starving. If

Maria wants to act like one of the guys at times, it is fine by me.

Dented Halos & Crooked Wings

There are certain times when a parent should allow their children to place dents in their halos, so the children do not feel as though their parent is trying to control every move they make. Nobody enjoys feeling like they are being controlled or micro-managed by another human being.

My mother told me when I became a teen that it is better for a parent to allow their children to be slightly naughty than it is for a parent to be too strict. She explained that when a parent is too strict that it can break a child's spirit, or an overly strict parent might inadvertently force their child to break the reigns and run wild. My mother explained her parenting philosophy to me when I was a young person because she did not want me to take advantage. I believe she was also training me to one day be a parent. I adopted my mother's philosophy and raised my children the same way.

It's good to coach our children often and provide them with guidance. After we have offered our guidance, we must step back and give our children enough breathing room to make the own decisions and their own mistakes. This approach has worked well with my children. Most of my children will confess to me when they've made a mistake or have done something wrong. They also snitch on each other, not to be malicious, but to look out for each other.

The main purpose of knowing what is going on in the lives of my children is to pray for them. I do not try to fix all their problems. However, I will reach out and offer some assistance when they are hurting, or they are feeling overwhelmed because I want them to know that I love them. It's my hope and prayer that the love they receive from me will give them the strength they need to recover from a setback, address their problem, and move forward.

Where I fall short in any aspect of my life, I hope Jesus, my Lord and Savior, will pick up the slack and fill in the gaps. God has already proven to me on numerous occasions that He has our backs!

Halo Hint

First-class angels trust in the Lord to fill the gaps and have our backs.

On that note, let's take a music break to listen to John Finch sing, "You Are Good" from his CD called Wildfire. Feel free to sing to the Lord with the song artist.

CHAPTER 9

Tales of a Comfort Food Queen

About nine months after my first marriage ended, a man showed up at my front door and said, "Ma'am, has anybody ever told you that you are a meat man's dream?"

I said, "Excuse me?"

He said, "I'm sorry for coming on strong, but when I was driving by your house, I happened to notice that you have both a refrigerator and a freestanding freezer in your garage. I would love to see the refrigerator inside your house."

Without warning, he barged through my front door and made his way down the hallway into my kitchen. My children were home, and I was alarmed that I had allowed an intruder to get past me. When he got into the kitchen, he hugged my refrigerator.

Then he said, "I knew you had a beautiful refrigerator before I even walked through the door. I love the way the wood panels match your cabinets. I'm sorry if I startled you, but I have a truck full of meat that I need to sell so I can pay for my daughter's tuition at a Catholic school. I know you're a Catholic because I saw the statue of Saint Francis of Assisi on your doorstep. I can tell that you're Italian, just by looking at you. I am Italian too, and I am going to make you an offer that you can't refuse! My wife is in the truck. Come outside. I want you to meet her."

I stood there in shock as the meat man gave me his sales pitch. When I followed him outside, I was pleasantly surprised to see his wife sitting in the passenger seat of the truck. At that moment, I realized that God had sent a first-class angel in the form of a meat man to my house to help me retain my right as *the custodial parent of my children* and retain my title as *the comfort food queen*, as I was going through a divorce! The meat man gave me a great deal on strip steaks marinated in butter. It became another one of our family favorites!

Halo Hint

Helping a single parent put good food on the table is an outstanding quality of a first-class angel.

One day when I was signing Charley up for baseball, a man who was about six and a half feet tall came up to me and said, "Ma'am, are you Charley's mother?"

I said, "Yes, I am."

He said, "Do you mind if I ask what you feed that boy?"

I said, "May I ask why you are asking?"

He said, "I just want to know what you feed that boy because your son played football against my boy, and your boy hurt my boy."

I said, "I am sorry my boy hurt your boy. My boy can be intense sometimes. He can't help it. He just wants to win."

The man said, "You don't understand. Nobody has ever hurt my boy before, and your boy made my boy cry! Your boy is a little boy. My boy is a big boy. Where does your little boy get his strength?"

I said, "I'm sorry Sir. I hope my son didn't hurt your son badly."

The man tipped his hat before he walked away and said, "Ma'am, you ought to be really proud of that boy!"

In addition to serving my children red meat and potatoes on a regular basis, I also served steamed broccoli and spinach drenched in olive oil and garlic. It's entirely possible that the greens made Charley as strong as Popeye, and his breath was bad enough to make a big boy cry!

About a year after I moved to Louisiana, Charley called me and said, "I already talked to the wrestling coach at Destrehan High School, and he said that he would be happy to have me on his team."

I said, "Are you serious? Do you want to move to Louisiana? Charley do you miss me or something?"

Charley said, "Yes, I miss you a lot, Mom!"

I said, "You do? Why?"

Charley said, "When I was hungry, you fed me. I could always count on you to make something that would hit the spot. Mom, they like to eat healthy over here, and I am always hungry."

I said, "There were so many times when I felt inadequate as a single mother. When all else failed, I did my best to cook with love. While you were quietly eating dinner and studying in the kitchen late in the evening, I usually washed the last pile of dishes left in the sink. It was a good way for the two of us to end the day. I miss you and the quiet time that we shared. I am happy that you miss me and want to live with me again, but I think you would regret moving away during your senior year of high school. You've only got one more year left before you go away to college, and then you'll be eating in the dorms. You won't have a personal chef at your beck and call. Living at your dad's house is good training for college."

(Charley was quietly listening. So, I kept chirping.)

"Besides, your wrestling coaches have worked hard with you throughout the years. It would not be fair to your coaches and your teammates in Illinois if you became a wrestling champion in the state of Louisiana.

"I also think you need to graduate from high school with your friends. Being friends with people you have known your entire life is a gift. You need to finish this chapter of your life with your childhood friends.

"On the weekends you can always take a ride over to Grandma Fran's house, Aunt Sue's house, or Aunt Jill's house. They'll be happy to give you something to eat that will stick to your ribs."

Charley said, "Mom, I think you're right. I'll finish out my senior year here in Illinois."

I was concerned about my older children after I moved away, but I knew I could count on my family and friends to serve as extra guardian angels in my absence. Many of our family members and friends had an open-door policy before I moved away. They served as sounding boards, mentors, and frequently invited my children over for dinner.

Halo Hint

Love, warmth, friendliness, hospitality, and generous self-giving are essential qualities of a first-class angel.

Bonus Halo Hint

It is good to write down our blessings, and the times God has answered our prayers. That way, we can reflect on them. Recalling our blessings keeps us anchored to God and helps us to trust the Lord when the storms of life engulf us like a raging tempest.

On that note, let's take a music break to listen to Rend Collective sing the song, "Counting Every Blessing."

CHAPTER 10

The Tempest

When Charley was in seventh grade, he told me that he was going to stop playing football, and he was going to start wrestling. When I asked him why he wanted to wrestle, he said, "I'd rather wrestle a guy my size than take a hit from a guy that is a lot bigger than me." At the time, I thought he had made a wise decision. Tommy joined the wrestling team with Charley but had no intention of giving up football.

After showing up to a handful of practices and wrestling meets, I couldn't help but notice that wrestling parents and coaches greeted me with enthusiasm. Tommy became a state championship qualifier the first year, and the enthusiasm of wrestling parents and coaches soared. Charley was not a state qualifier the first year, but he received a trophy for "Most Improved Wrestler."

After he saw his older brother go to state the first year, Charley boasted to everybody that he was going to the state championship the next year and come in first place. He looked like a pee-wee compared to the other kids in the seventh grade. Everybody chuckled and found his bloated level of self-confidence amusing. Charley gained everybody's respect and admiration when his prediction came true, and he came in first place at the state championship in eighth grade.

The first two years of wrestling were exciting for my sons and all members of our family. It was around the third year of wrestling that my enthusiasm evaporated. There were too many times when my sons came home from wrestling and looked like they had been in a street fight. They got many facial abrasions. Wrestling broke Charley's perfect nose and caused Tommy and Charley to get cauliflower ear. Those injuries were traumatizing to me, but they only intensified my sons' desire to win wrestling meets and go to the state championship every year of high school.

After my two younger sons, Johnny and Tony, saw their older brothers win many medals and go to state championships, the day arrived when they decided that they wanted to wrestle. Participating in sports is great fun for young people, but I would have been happier if my younger sons had chosen to swim and play tennis.

When I went home to visit my family on the weekend of my daughter's college graduation, Charley never looked worse to me.

I said, "Charley! You look horrible! What happened to you?"

Not only did he have a blackened eye, but the blood vessels in his eye were broken.

Charley said, "I accidentally head-butted another wrestler during a wrestling conference last weekend. I also had the flu, but I feel great! Mom, I came in first place at the freestyle championship! The wrestling coaches from Northwestern University were there. They want me to join their team!"

Charley was excited that his victory at the end of his senior year captured the attention of the wrestling coaches at Northwestern, a university in the Chicago area that competes against Ivy League schools in sports and academics. Unfortunately, Charley looked so beat up that I couldn't bask with him in his glory.

I said, "Are you sure you only had the flu, and you didn't have a concussion?"

Charley said, "Mom, I'm fine. Don't worry. The flu is going around at school. My step-brother had it too."

Four days later, Charley had his first seizure. Before he arrived at the nearest hospital, he had another seizure. He had more seizures that very same evening after being admitted to the hospital.

Nobody had the heart to call me when Charley started having seizures. When his father phoned later the next day, he told me Charley had a few seizures. He also told me not to worry, that it wasn't as bad as it seemed.

I asked Allen what caused the seizures. He told me the doctors hadn't arrived at a conclusion. Intuition told me Charley had a concussion a few days before. However, the shock of the bad news wiped out that part of my memory.

Allen was a former paramedic. I was confident that he could assess the situation and make the right decisions for our son until I could get back to Chicago.

At the time, Joe and I were in the process of moving from southern Louisiana to northern Louisiana. I had already created a delay with our move when I attended my daughter's college graduation in Illinois the weekend before Charley started having seizures. Johnny, one of my younger sons, was about to graduate from eighth grade. There was a list of tasks that I needed to do so we could move, and Joe could start his new job on time.

I found myself in a fretful state of paralysis and was worried that if I showed up at the hospital in a state of panic that it would cloud Allen's judgment. My feelings of alarm increased when I did not receive an update on Charley's condition the following day. I called Allen, but there was no answer. Then I called Maria and asked how her brother was doing. I could tell that she was selecting her words carefully. To extract more information, I asked her what it was like when Charley had a seizure. She told me that he would stare out into space and a blank look would come over his face. After each spell, he would fall asleep. I had worked as a medical secretary for three neurologists many years before. I knew Maria description of Charley's seizures placed them in the category of "petit mal." I took a deep breath, and I asked the question that I did not want to ask, "Did your brother have any grand mal seizures?"

As though she had been permitted to unload a heavy burden, she said firmly, "Yes, the first two were grand mal seizures."

My heart sank to the floor. I said, "Maria, is my son going to be okay?"

Maria became very choked up and said, "I don't know, Mom! This is scary! Nobody wants you to see Charley in this condition, but I think you need to get here as soon as you can!"

She broke down and sobbed uncontrollably for about a minute. When Maria regained her composure, she explained that a nurse at the hospital had given Charley a muffin to eat after he complained of hunger. While he was eating, he had a third grand mal seizure. It was so violent that Maria and her father helped two other nurses hold him down.

Halo Hint

The willingness and ability to assist during a crisis is an admirable quality of a first-class angel.

I asked Maria if I could speak to Charley. She told me he was asleep. I decided to stop at a church to light a candle and asked a priest to pray with me. When we were done praying, Father John Bosco told me that I was going to be on a long journey with my son. I finally got to speak to Charley right before sundown. He sounded good under the conditions. I was happy and relieved to hear his voice.

When I spoke to Allen, he told me Charley's blood tests came out negative. The brain scans showed that Charley's brain had some slight swelling, but there were no lesions or tumors. He informed me that he arranged to have Charley transferred to a hospital, located in downtown Chicago. Then Allen told me that Charley had too many seizures and to pray that the doctors would get them under control. After I hung up the phone, I told Joe that I had to go to Chicago to see my son.

As I was boarding the plane, I found out that the doctors had already decided to place Charley in a medically induced coma to calm the storm taking place inside his brain. When I walked into the hospital room a few hours later, my son had a tube shoved down his throat, IVs in his arm, and electrodes stuck to his matted hair. He had already been in a medically induced coma for about six hours. His body was twitching and making spastic movements.

I asked a nurse, "Is my son having a seizure right now?"

She said, "No, he is not having a seizure. We will tell you if the doctors detect another one from the EEG. The twitching and spasms happen more frequently when a person has a lot of muscle mass. Athletes metabolize medication faster than most people. Your son's body is fighting the sedation. We will gradually increase the sedation. After a while, his body will stop having spasms."

Having watched too many movies, I said, "Wait a minute! The doctors aren't going to flat-line my son's brain, are they?"

The nurse said, "Oh no! Your son will still have brain waves. However, we are slowing down the electrical impulses in his brain with the hope that it will reset his brain and stop the storm that is taking place inside of his brain."

Charley's body stopped twitching and making sporadic movements a few hours later. It seemed like he was barely alive. However, his quiet, peaceful presence made it easier for me to pray.

The next day the doctors informed us that they would not take Charley out of the medically induced coma until he was seizure-free for at least twenty-four hours. His sedation was so heavy that there was no way we could tell when he was having a seizure. Every so often a nurse would enter his room and give us the bad news that the doctors had detected another seizure on the EEG. Charley continued to have seizures at least once a day for several days even though he was receiving extremely high doses of seizure medication while in a medically induced coma.

Family members sat by Charley's side around the clock. We paired up at night and stayed with him in shifts. One of us always tried to remain awake, keep watch, and pray for Charley.

Charley was continuously evaluated by medical doctors who were monitoring the electrical nerve impulses of his brain with an EEG from another hospital room during the day, or from their homes at night. We learned that no news throughout the night didn't necessarily mean that we would hear good news in the morning. There were times when we got our hopes up too high when we thought Charley had gone twenty-four hours without a seizure, only to learn from the morning crew that Charley had yet another seizure between midnight and sunrise.

Halo Hint

Remaining steadfast in prayer, even when it seems like the Lord is not answering our prayers,

is an important aspect of a first-class angel's job description.

On that note, let's take a music break to listen to Lauren Daigle sing, "Trust in You."

CHAPTER 11

Advanced Halo Hints

Joe tied up all the loose ends and finalized all the arrangements for our move while I was in Chicago. He also made the long drive to Chicago with my two younger sons, after they got out of school for the summer. Joe's reliability and his ability to handle a lot of pressure are just some of the qualities that make him a first-class angel and winner at the game of life and love!

Halo Hint

Reliability, and the ability to manage projects while under a great deal of pressure are outstanding qualities of a first-class angel.

Even though it was difficult to celebrate anything, we went ahead and celebrated my son Johnny's eighth-grade graduation with many family members at The Rose Bud Café, an Italian restaurant on Taylor Street in Chicago's "Little Italy." We had to try to remain positive and celebrate during this storm of life, especially considering the fact it was the year of the "Trifecta of Graduations" in my family. I was the proud mother of three graduates that year. One from eighth grade, one from high school, and one from college -- all with straight A's!

Even though Charley couldn't finish out the year, the teachers gave him straight A's based on his performance throughout high school. It was another cause for celebration. Naturally, I was proud of my children's hard work and accomplishments.

A few of Charley's high school friends came to visit him the same evening that we went to The Rosebud Café. One of his teammates broke down and cried when he saw Charley. His tears caused a chain reaction among Charley's friends. I hugged the kids and told them that Charley was going to be okay.

While Charley was in the medically induced coma, I did my best to hope for the best possible outcome. I was able to keep a positive mindset thanks to Christian authors and public speakers such as Joel Osteen, Stormie Omartian, and my other brothers and sisters in Christ who have taught me how to exercise my faith in God by believing in positive outcomes and saying positive things even in dire situations.

The easiest way to keep a positive mindset is to focus on Jesus words, "for God all things are possible." (Matthew 19:26) God also said in Jeremiah 32:27, "Is anything too difficult for me?" Jesus also told us in Mark 11:24 that when we pray, we should always believe that God will meet our needs. It is always better to express our faith in what we hope God can do for us (accomplish the impossible) than to express our worries and doubts.

Halo Hint

Maintaining a positive outlook, saying positive things, and guarding our tongue against negativity, even during the darkest moments, is an essential part of a first-class angel's job description.

A Thank-You Note

I want to express my gratitude for the hard work and dedication of the doctors, nurses, and technicians that worked with Charley while he was in the hospital. Thank you for listening to God's call on your life to save people's lives. All of you are first-class angels and winners at the game of life and love in my book.

I also want to thank Charley's friends for visiting Charley while he was in the hospital. Each of you specially blessed us with your presence and the gift of your tears. Tears do not flow from my eyes as often as I would like. It is for that reason that I treasured the gift of your tears. I am aware of Washington Irving's words that "There is a sacredness in tears. They are not the mark of weakness, but of power. They speak more eloquently than ten thousand tongues. They are messengers of overwhelming grief, of deep contrition, and unspeakable love."

I want all of Charley's friends to know that you rose to the occasion through your loving concern and support. That makes all of you first-class angels and winners at the game of life and love in my book!

Several of Charley's family members, my friends, wrestling coaches, and parents of his teammates also visited Charley while he was in the hospital. I want to thank you too. You all are first-class angels of moral support and winners at the game of life and love! Thank you for being there for us when we needed you the most.

Halo Hint

Offering moral support during a crisis and expressing one's love and concern are important aspects of a first-class angel's job description.

I counted my blessings while my son was in a medically induced coma and stepped away another evening to celebrate my second wedding anniversary with Joe. The two of us went to Navy Pier, a beautiful site on Lake Michigan in Chicago. It gave me a much needed mental break, and it was therapeutic to watch the sunset during a time of immense stress.

Though Joe did not express his disappointment, my son's medical crisis was a downer for Joe for more than one reason. For one, the joy that would typically accompany the purchase of a newly-married couple's first home got derailed by my son's medical crisis. Moreover, Joe had already served as a support beam for me when I had a medical crisis of my own during our first wedding anniversary. The joy of our first wedding anniversary, as well as our second one, was overshadowed by the heavy clouds that accompanied the storms of life. Within the first two years of marriage, Joe showed me that he loves me in good times and bad, in sickness, in health, and during times of crisis. I am sad to say that we had more bad times than good times during our first two years of marriage. There was more than one train wreck, but Joe endured it like a champ! Thank you, Joe, for being a first-class angel!

Halo Hint

Loving someone in sickness and health and being someone's support beam during times of crisis are important aspects of every first-class angel's job description.

Even though I could not shake off all my worries during my sons' medical crisis, I have been fascinated with the idea of dancing and singing in the rain for most of my life. My fascination goes all the way back to my early childhood when I saw an academy-award winning musical with Gene Kelly called, "Singin' in the Rain." I do not remember the storyline, but I have never forgotten the chorus and the melody of that song.

On that note let's take a music break to listen to Gene Kelly sing the song, "Singin' in the Rain." Also, note that the white sound from the rain and the sound of Gene Kelly tap dancing is both delightful and therapeutic.

In recent times Jack Vettriano's oil painting called "The Singing Butler" is a work of art that has caught the attention of people across the globe. It is an iconic painting of a man and woman dressed in formal attire, dancing on the beach during a rainstorm. The woman is wearing a red evening gown with a low-cut back that reveals her curves and well-maintained body. She is wearing long red gloves that cover most of her arm. The man is wearing a black suit and a white shirt. Their attire suggests that the couple is well-to-do, as does the fact that they have a maid and a butler to accompany them on their journey. The couple is dancing close together, wrapped in each other's arms. They are serene and happy as they dance in the storm. The woman's muscles in her shoulders and upper arms seem to convey the message that she has a lot of strength and resilience. However, she doesn't seem to mind leaning on the man she loves as they dance during the storm of life. The man and the woman are strong when they are apart, but their love for each other makes them stronger.

In my eyes, the man and women symbolize a power couple that is winning the game of life and love. Nothing, not even the storms of life, can drag them down. The maid and the butler remind us of loving service to others during the storms of life.

The Singing Butler is Britain's most famous work of art, and numerous reprints of the painting have been made and distributed throughout the world. The picture began speaking to me the first time I saw it. Now that I live in a state threatened by seasonal hurricanes, the painting talks to me even more.

The butler can be seen holding up an umbrella, shielding the couple from "the storm of life." Based on the name of the painting, we know that the butler is singing to the couple as they dance on the beach. The couple dancing in the rain is the primary focus of the painting. However, the butler represents a first-class angel and a winner in the game of life and love due to his ability to take care of other people's needs during the storms of life.

The maid seems to be a little too preoccupied with her own needs, while she holds up an umbrella over her head and attempts to prevent her white cap from being blown away during the storm. She also appears to be more distressed by the storm than the dancing couple or the singing butler. She hasn't yet learned how to sing and dance during the storms of life. If she pays attention, she can learn an important lesson from the others' example.

However, the maid might be the voice of reason, telling the others that they need to seek shelter before all the hotels get booked up for the evening. There is a little bag that can be seen by the maid's feet. It gives me the impression that the maid anticipated everybody's needs when she packed a bag of toiletries for everybody before the couple lost all their worldly possessions during the storm of life.

Perhaps the main reason the couple can dance during the storm of life is that they have experienced many storms together, and they are confident that they have what it takes to get through another one and recover from it. Being forced to start over again, might help the couple feel as though they are newlyweds, just starting out in life.

Perhaps the couple also realizes that although the storm has destroyed all their possessions, their love for each other is what they treasure the most. They also possess the love, loyalty, and friendship of two people who have become like family to them.

Halo Hints

Love, loyalty, and friendship are gifts of priceless value. These priceless gifts should always be treasured and never taken for granted. The best way to show true appreciation for these beautiful gifts is to be a giver and not just a receiver of the gifts.

Singing or dancing during the storms of life is a theme that appeals to people across the continents. There have been many times in my life when I utilized singing and dancing as a form of therapy when I experienced sadness, heartbreak, and other forms of stress.

Unfortunately, I must admit that there have been times when I had no idea what to do during a time of crisis or what I should do to help other people during their time of crisis. I can relate to the maid in "The Singing Butler" more than the other three people in the painting. I am not good at being a first-responder. It does not come naturally to me. My mind shuts down during the initial shock of a major crisis. Even after the initial shock has subsided, my brain processes things slowly for quite a while, which in turn causes me to be a late responder. Also, my initial attempt to help during a crisis might be on a small scale just like the maid who provided a small bag of toiletries.

Being a late responder is not a horrible character flaw especially when we consider that it usually takes a long time for people to recover from a crisis. People may still be recovering from a disaster for months or years after the initial shock of it has diminished for those who were not directly affected by the crisis. Late responders can offer prayer support and moral support for as long as it takes people to put the pieces of their lives back together. There is a great need for early responders and late responders during the storms of life.

Halo Hint

Responding to the needs of others during the height of a crisis or helping people to recover during the aftermath of a crisis are important aspects of a first-class angel's job description.

It does not matter if we are early responders or late responder. Any act of kindness serves as a blessing to those in crisis. People usually appreciate all the help and prayer support that they can get when the storms of life have blown them down. Just knowing that there are people in this world that truly care about them gives them the strength that they need to rise above a tragedy.

One of the best things anybody can do to relieve someone's distress is to hug them. Striving to be an expert hug-therapist is a loving way to respond to people during a crisis.

Halo Hint

Providing hug therapy is an important aspect of a first-class angel's job description.

A big part of learning how to sing or dance in the rain has something to do with the way people come together during a crisis, even when people do not get along with each other. I was anxious about having to spend time with Allen at the hospital. He and I got along better when we did not spend time together. Through the grace of God, Allen and I ended the cold war while Charley was in a medically induced coma.

Halo Hint

Working cooperatively together (and sometimes in shifts) during a crisis is an important aspect of a first-class angel's job description.

I was grateful to Allen for taking the night shift with our son on the evening of my second wedding anniversary with Joe. This gesture of kindness stood out to me because it was performed by the same man who got upset with me for going into labor on a Sunday evening at the end of the Thanksgiving holiday when I was giving birth to Charley. Allen made up for that faux pas many years later when he responded to our son's needs during his medical crisis and numerous times in the aftermath of the crisis. Allen possesses the qualities that make him a first-class angel of a father and a winner at the game of life and love.

Bonus Halo Hints

- **Find a quiet place to ask God to enlighten our minds, so we will have a better idea of how to respond during a crisis or the aftermath of a crisis.**

- **Pray for the person or the group of people in distress, that God will give them the strength and endurance to recover from a crisis.**

- **Sing songs of praise to the Lord.**

We can follow the example of King David who wrote the Psalms in the Bible and sang to the Lord during the high notes and low notes of life. Singing and worshiping the Lord filled him with strength and joy in both good times and bad. (Psalms 118:14)

Saint Augustine of Hippo, the great Christian philosopher, is believed to have said, "He who sings once, prays twice." During the storms of life, we can offer the Lord a song of praise not only for the victim(s) but ourselves and for all those who will respond to the crisis.

CHAPTER 12

The Aftermath of the Storm

After Charley had been in a medically induced coma for about eleven days, a specialist recommended a procedure called plasmapheresis to cleanse Charley's blood of antibodies. Although Charley's blood tests showed up normal before he had the plasmapheresis treatments, it was as though he responded to the treatments when the seizures finally came to a halt!

The doctors decided to wait closer to forty-eight hours before they took Charley out of the medically induced coma. A nurse informed us that under the circumstances, we could expect that Charley would experience amnesia as a side effect of the seizures and the medically induced coma that could be temporary or permanent.

We were unwilling to accept what the nurse said to us because we were hoping and praying for a miracle. We were so hopeful that we allowed Charley's high school to arrange for him to give the commencement speech from his hospital bed through a live video. Everyone on our end believed that one way or another Charley was going to be a part of his graduation ceremony.

Shortly after Charley became conscious, he asked us what day it was and told us that he wanted to leave the hospital to attend his graduation. He was also able to recall that he had been selected to give a commencement speech to his graduating class, and he wanted to give it. Unfortunately, it was as though an imposter hijacked his voice.

He did not sound like the same person. It was shocking and alarming for us to listen to the way he was speaking. For that reason, we didn't allow him to read his speech from his hospital bed on the day of his graduation. We did not tell him that we had even considered it.

Charley broke down and cried when we told him that he would not be able to leave the hospital to attend his graduation. Even sadder and more traumatic for everyone was that his graduation ceremony was taking place just as he was waking up. We choked back the tears as we broke the news to him. However, the fact that he could even remember that he was supposed to give a speech to his graduating class was very good regarding his prognosis. Though he did not realize it, Charley was at his graduation ceremony, at least in spirit. One of his friends served as his proxy and gave Charley's speech on his behalf. The theme of his speech was about the graduates flying from the nest. Sadly, Charley was the only who failed to launch that year. At least he lived when he tried to flap his wings and proceeded to fall from the nest!

Every so often, I come across a commencement speech that inspires me. Denzel Washington gave an excellent speech to graduates at Dillard University in New Orleans. The type of speech that he gave is not common at colleges. I ask you to look it up.

It was apparent by the speech that he gave that Denzel Washington must have picked up a Bible and read it a time or two. Jesus tells us to seek first the kingdom of God, and his righteousness, and we will be blessed. (Matthew 6:33 paraphrased)

Halo Hint

Putting God first is the most important part of a first-class angel's job description. It lines up with our main mission, "to create a little piece of Heaven on Earth in our neck of the woods!"

At times, the Lord disciplines the ones He loves, just as we are told in Hebrews 12:6 and Proverbs 3:12. The discipline is not meant to be a punishment, but more of a wakeup call. Whether we realize it or not, every blessing and every cross is designed to draw us closer to God. Nothing happens to us that God did not foresee before He formed us in our mother's womb.

When my son ended up in the hospital at the end of his senior year in high school, I thought God was trying to get my son's attention by sending him a heavy cross to carry, and that God was trying to get him to move in a different direction than what he had chosen for himself. I thought Jesus was knocking loudly on the door of my son's heart. When Jesus knocks, we won't know what He wants until we open the door and listen to Him. It's important to pray for discernment of God's call and open our ears during the storms of life.

Although Charley's brain was in the hibernation mode for two weeks, there was still a part of his brain that remembered that he had big plans. Moreover, he had enough wits about him to realize that a serious medical condition foiled his plans. As a result, his sadness swiftly gave way to rage. He started shouting, "Why did this have to happen? Why God, why?"

My son did not understand why God sent him such a big cross to carry. Charley reminded me of the apostles who had their own preconceived ideas about how life "is supposed to be" and did not readily understand the lessons that Jesus taught them.

Charley possessed an incredible amount of upper body strength even though his weight dropped down to about ninety-two pounds. His coordination was very poor, and he started flailing his arms and legs around like an oversized baby beast to get out of the hospital bed. He kept trying to flip his entire body out of the bed until he wore himself out. As soon as he regained some of his strength, he would try to flip himself out of bed once again. My poor son kept begging us to untie him. His father and I could not stand seeing him tied to the hospital bed after staring at his nearly lifeless body caused by a medically induced coma for two weeks. So, we decided to wrestle with him to provide him with some relief from the ropes that held him bound to the bed. In retrospect, it was a grave mistake. Wrestling with Charley only served as a reminder that he was a wrestler, the one thing I was hoping he would forget!

CHAPTER 13

A Long Road to Recovery

It was a relief when Charley finally calmed down after two days and nights of putting up a huge fight. He was sincerely sorry for the profanity and many of the things he said while he was in a state of rage. He was also most embarrassed that he had become dependent on his family members and the nurses to help him do the things that he usually did for himself.

In a matter of seven days, I saw my son develop from someone who was like a giant baby beast to a child who had not yet gone through puberty but still did not know how to walk. When people asked how he was doing, I felt the need to withhold information. The seriousness of my son's condition was too difficult for me to discuss even with some of my closest friends.

The doctors provided my son with the diagnosis of "autoimmune encephalitis." However, I still wanted the doctors to explain what caused my son to have seizures. After I asked, the doctors and residents remained silent and did not answer my question.

I said, "I already know you were only treating my son's symptoms. That's what one of the doctors told me a few weeks ago. Nonetheless, I would like somebody to determine the major cause of my son's seizures. A person's brain does not decide to go haywire for no reason whatsoever. Even if Charley had some antibodies circulating throughout his bloodstream that his blood tests failed to reveal, there must be an underlying reason for that too. The body doesn't attack itself for no reason whatsoever. Are you sure it wasn't my son's eye injury that caused my son to have seizures?"

There was silence as I held up a picture of Charley's eye that he posted on his Facebook page right after he won the freestyle wrestling championship a week and a half before he had his first grand mal seizure.

I had made a conscious effort not to spend a lot of time on social media while Charley was in the hospital except to ask friends and family to pray for him. For that reason, I didn't see the photo of my son's eye injury until he was about to be released from the hospital. As soon as I saw the photo, my mind flashed back to what he looked like on the day Maria graduated. When I saw Charley in person that day, it had already been an entire week after he head-butted his opponent. His eye was still badly bruised, and the blood vessels in his eye were still broken. His eye injury looked a lot worse in the photo than what it looked like when I saw him in person, a week after his eye was injured.

While Charley was in a medically induced coma, I listened to family members and doctors discuss my son's medical condition. Many people brought up valid points which caused me to believe that many factors caused the perfect storm in my son's brain. By the time Charley was ready to be released from the hospital, his eye injury stood out to me more than anything.

After I asked if the eye injury was the cause of my son's seizures, one doctor broke the silence and said, "Your son responded to plasmapheresis, which is why we provided him with the diagnosis of autoimmune encephalitis."

I said, "A lot of people were praying for my son. We don't know if it was the power of everyone's prayers that stopped his seizures or the plasmapheresis treatments. We are willing to accept your diagnosis, so he can be transferred from this hospital to the next hospital to receive therapy. However, I still need someone from this hospital to tell me if my son's eye injury caused the seizures."

Nobody responded, but I sensed they were mulling it over after they saw the photo of my son's eye injury.

Halo Hint

There are times when a first-class angel must speak up and ask the right questions with the hope of getting the right answers during or after a crisis.

The next morning a nurse practitioner told me that it would be beneficial for me to attend a special forum in which I would get to meet a world-renowned physician who was going to provide a presentation that might assist us with my son's care after he was released from the hospital. What I didn't realize until after I showed up to the forum was that one of the brain specialists at the hospital had taken an interest in my son's case and wanted to discuss it with the neurology students.

If someone had come right out and asked me to participate in a case study, I would have gladly accepted the invitation. Having been a former medical secretary at Northwestern Medical School in the Department of Neurology many years before, I was familiar with case studies because I was the secretary who often was asked to type up the notes from the case studies.

When I was a medical secretary back in my twenties, I was the quiet mouse that sat in the background, just like the mice in the laboratory. I felt honored to participate in a case study. More importantly, I wanted to spend time discussing my son's case with a medical doctor before Charley left the hospital. I was grateful that God provided me with a perfect opportunity.

The brain specialist asked me to share my son's medical history from the time he was a child up until he started having seizures.

I said, "Charley never had any major illnesses from the time he was a baby. He seemed to have had the strongest constitution of any member of our family because he rarely came down with a cold or the flu. When he was a child, he got a small cut in the cuticle of his finger. We were in Colorado skiing, and we didn't know about his small cut. His ski gloves caused an infection to spread quickly, and we brought him to the emergency room. They placed him on an antibiotic.

"He has a lawn maintenance business, and he has had poison ivy many times. Charley started wrestling in seventh grade. He has experienced ringworm a few times too. He also suffers from acne in that his face is constantly rubbing against the mats. I noticed that his skin has cleared up beautifully since being in the hospital. Many of his conditions have been skin-related.

"Due to wrestling, his nose has been broken, and he has cauliflower ear. To the best of my knowledge, he never had a concussion except for the time I suspected one when I saw him at my daughter's graduation, one week after he head-butted his opponent and injured his eye at a freestyle wrestling championship.

"When I saw my son in person a week after his injury, all the blood vessels in his eye were still broken. However, he was in good spirits because he had won the freestyle championship, and that's when the coaches at Northwestern University discovered him."

I held up Charley's photo from Facebook and said, "As you can see from his photo, he was very happy. His skin tone is bright and vibrant in this picture. By the time I saw my son in person a week later, his skin tone was dull and gray. According to my calculations, approximately twelve days had passed from the time my son head-butted his opponent to the time he had his first grand mal seizure.

"Charley was also under a tremendous amount of stress the day before he started having seizures. He has a lawn maintenance business, and he had just finished taking some of his final exams. He was filling out the registration and financial forms to attend Northwestern University at the last minute. He was in a state of panic when I spoke to him on the phone the night before the seizures began. When I googled seizures, I noticed that high levels of stress are one of the triggers for seizure activity.

"To make matters worse, Charley hit his head on a piece of equipment at his father's fitness center a few minutes before he had the first grand mal seizure when he was goofing around doing flips. He was happy and excited about many things because his life was on the upswing.

"Everybody who saw Charley stumble and hit his head said it seemed like a minor accident. However, he had his first grand mal seizure a few minutes later. There were no visible signs of bumps or bruises from the second head injury. The CT and MRI revealed only slight swelling of his brain."

The doctor said, "I believe the most significant thing that happened to your son was the eye injury."

I said, "I had a feeling that it was significant. It's just that I don't understand how it was significant when the brain scans indicated that my son's brain experienced very little swelling."

The doctor said, "There is no bone and no cartilage that serves as a protective barrier between the eye and the brain, and there are numerous nerves in the eye that connect to the brain. Nerve damage most likely occurred even though the brain scans detected swelling that was so slight that it almost seemed insignificant."

The brain specialist directed his attention to the students and said, "We always need to give eye injuries serious consideration especially when a neurological condition presents itself."

Then he stood up and provided a short demonstration, using a student's head. The doctor said, "Nerve damage could travel from one side of the brain to the other side of the brain. Nerve damage could also take place in the center of the brain or on a diagonal. Much is dependent on the angle and impact of the blow."

I asked, "Why didn't the doctors find any nerve damage on Charley's CT and MRI?"

The doctor said, "The medical world does not have any diagnostic tools available to detect nerve damage because the nerves are too minuscule. The best way to detect nerve damage is to give a patient a neuropsychological exam. Your son has not had one yet. We need to give his brain a few more weeks to heal before we provide one. It will establish a baseline. He will need another neuropsychological exam in six months to see how he is progressing."

I said, "What are the chances that my son will recover?"

He said, "Your son has been through a lot, but he has youth on his side. His brain will continue to develop until he is about thirty years old. If any parts of his brain are injured, the neuropathways in his brain will reroute themselves, and he will be able to do many of the same things that he did before.

"By the way, is your son just into wrestling or is there anything else that he enjoys doing?"

I said, "He concentrated mostly on school, wrestling, and his lawn maintenance business. He also has some close friends.

The doctor asked, "What were his favorite subjects?"

I said, "Math and physics. He won't have to take any math in college. He took advanced placement classes and tested out of all of them."

The doctor said, "Your son is going to have to take things slow for a while. It might best for him to go to a community college in the fall and ease back into academics."

I said, "My son is not going to be happy. He has his heart set on attending Northwestern University in the fall."

He said, "The high achievers are the ones who usually have the hardest time coping with brain injuries."

I asked, "I believe that he will push himself hard to recover. After he does, will he be able to wrestle?"

He said, "It is in your son's best interest to retire from wrestling. He needs to do everything in his power to protect his brain from future injuries."

I said, "I agree. I've been waiting for a doctor to tell us that he should not wrestle. Would you consult with my son and provide him with your opinion?"

He said, "Yes, I will stop by to see him tomorrow."

I sighed with relief. I wanted at least one doctor to address my concern before Charley left the hospital. I thanked God that the doctor miraculously entered the picture.

The doctor's desire to educate the medical students and me by sharing his knowledge with us makes him a first-class angel and winner at the game of life and love.

Halo Hint

Sharing one's knowledge and expertise are important aspects of a first-class angel's job description.

Additional Shockwaves

As promised the brain specialist consulted with Charley and told him that he should retire from wrestling.

Charley protested, "Wrestling is not a dangerous sport! It's a lot less dangerous than football! I love wrestling!"

The doctor said, "Normally, wrestling is less dangerous than football. Son, your brain has experienced enough trauma for one lifetime. It's time for you to retire from wrestling. You must do everything in your power to protect your brain from future injuries."

Charley's eyes welled up with tears as the doctor walked out of his room. One minute had not passed when his high school wrestling coach knocked on the door. Charley began sobbing and asked me to leave the room. As I was standing in the hallway, Allen showed up too. I had not breathed a word to Allen about the conversation that I had with the brain specialist during the case study, or that I had asked the brain specialist to speak to Charley about retiring from wrestling. Allen wanted to know why Charley was so upset. I did my best to provide him with a summary of what the doctor and I discussed and what the doctor told Charley.

Allen said, "I want to see Charley. I'll talk to you later."

After Allen assessed the situation, he told me that he was worried that the bad news from the brain specialist had pushed Charley over the edge.

I said, "I knew Charley would be upset, but not enough to take his own life. Are you concerned that he would do something that drastic?"

Allen said, "Yes, I am! You heard him saying all kinds of irrational things when he came out of the coma. He was just starting to settle down and wrap his mind around what happened. It was a mistake to tell the doctor to speak to him so soon."

I said, "He has to start processing that he has to retire from wrestling while there are professionals available to help him work through his loss."

Allen said, "That doctor that you spoke to is the only doctor on staff who thinks our son should not wrestle again. The rest of the doctors have said that it is too soon to tell whether or not Charley could wrestle again."

I said, "Any doctor who says our son might be able to wrestle again is insane!"

Allen said, "You're not a doctor, and it's not your judgment call to make. It would help if you had spoken to me before you told the doctor to speak to Charley. It was not right for you to go over my head! Charley is living with me now, not with you!"

I said, "I have been sitting quietly in the corner ever since I arrived at this hospital. I have patiently waited for the doctors to tell us what caused the seizures until two days ago when I found the picture of Charley's eye injury on Facebook. I suspected wrestling had something to do with Charley's seizures the entire time I've been here. I didn't want to speak to you about it because it was just as hard for me to burst your bubble as it was for me to burst Charley's bubble. Do you think I have not noticed how much you two have bonded as father and son ever since Charley started wrestling? However, when I saw the picture of Charley's eye injury on Facebook, it confirmed my suspicions that wrestling contributed to his seizures. I believe our son needs to retire from wrestling, and there is a doctor on staff who specializes in brain injuries who stated that Charley should give it up."

Allen said, "Are you saying that you agree with one doctor on staff, instead of all the other specialists on staff who have said that it is too soon to tell?"

I said, "Yes. I trust this doctor's opinion more than any other doctor on staff because he's older and has more experience than all of them."

Allen said, "The doctor who decided to give Charley plasmapheresis treatments is brilliant. He said it is too soon to say whether or not Charley could wrestle again, and he thinks Charley's prognosis is very good!"

I said, "He believes an autoimmune issue is the cause of the seizures. One of the nurses told us that the doctors use that diagnosis when they don't know for certain what caused the symptoms. The brain specialist I spoke with said his eye injury stood out to him more than anything else because there are so many nerves in the eye that connect to the brain."

Allen said, "I disagree. If the nerves in his eye are damaged, wouldn't it affect his vision? I think Charley's seizures had more to do with his diet and all the stress that he was under."

I said, "I'm sure many things played a role in creating the perfect storm in Charley's brain, but we cannot rule out his eye injury or wrestling. His head has been jostled and knocked around numerous times throughout the years, and we can't allow it to keep happening!"

Allen said, "I want Charley to do everything that he planned on doing before he ended up in the hospital. Charley loves wrestling, and he wants to wrestle at Northwestern. Taking away his dreams will do a lot more harm than good! All the doctors have said his prognosis is good because he has youth on his side. If Charley is still smart enough to figure out a way to wrestle, I am not going to stop him. I'm not going to take away his dream!

"Besides, I don't want Charley doing something that is going to be a lot worse for him than wrestling. He's going to be eighteen. We won't be able to watch every move that he makes after he leaves the hospital. If he starts drinking or doing drugs with the medication that he has to take for seizures, how good will that be for his brain? He could end up killing himself if he mixes that medication with other drugs or alcohol. Wrestling has done a great job of keeping Charley drug and alcohol-free. I've got enough relatives who have messed up their lives or have ended up dead because of drugs and alcohol. Charley is more likely to take care of his health and do well in school if he wrestles."

It was disheartening that I couldn't convince Allen that Charley needed to stop wrestling. There are no words to express how much I regretted that I had not allowed Charley to move to Louisiana when he asked to move in with me right before his senior year. He wouldn't have had to fight as hard to win a championship. He might not have gotten an eye injury or seizures if he had wrestled in Louisiana during his senior year of high school.

In spite of the misery I felt, my conversation with the brain specialist and Charley's father was an eye-opening experience for me. I began to realize like never before that everyone's brains are wired differently. The way one person processes information can be completely different than the way another person processes the same information. Not being wired the same way is the reason doctors can disagree with each other, possess different opinions, and arrive at different conclusions. Not being wired the same way is the reason married couples and former spouses can disagree and have different opinions. Once we realize that we are all wired differently, we do not have to get angry when we have an opinion that is different than others. However, it is important to make a genuine attempt to listen to the other person's perspective. If we fail to do that, we can never hope to have a meeting of the minds.

Even though many of us are wired differently, there are times when we must put our minds together to come up with the best solution in a difficult situation, especially when there is not a perfect solution. In some cases, our inability to arrive at a mutual understanding can end up being a matter of life or death for someone or a group of people.

When Allen left the hospital, I went back into Charley's room with the hope of reprogramming his brain.

I said, "Charley, I know wrestling means the world to you, but I want to tell you a story about an old childhood friend of mine. Her name was Angela. She was one of my very dearest friends. She was told by her doctor when she was in her late twenties not to have a second child due to a health problem that she had. Having two children, a boy and a girl, was something that she wanted from the time we were kids. My friend did not want to give up her dream, and she decided to have a second child against her doctor's orders. Unfortunately, she died two months after she gave birth to her baby girl.

"When my friend told me that she was going to try to have another baby, I didn't want her to give up her dream of having two children. I truly believed that she would defy the odds and never thought something bad was going to happen to her. When she died, I learned that we are only made of flesh and blood."

Charley said, "I don't care Mom! I love wrestling! I would rather die than not wrestle. I wish you understood how much I love wrestling!"

I said, "You need to allow your love for wrestling to die! It is toxic love. It's not a love worth keeping. You must find a new love!"

Charley said, "Mom, I need to get some rest. You can leave now if you want."

I said, "Close your eyes and get some rest. Go ahead. I'm not stopping you."

That's when I got on Facebook, and I noticed that I received a note from Angela's son, asking me if he could read the book that I had written about his mom. It sent chills up and down my spine!

The last time I had seen Angela's son was when I briefly introduced myself to him as an old friend of his mother's when he was about seven years old. On a whim, I tried to friend him on Facebook a few weeks before my son was admitted to the hospital.

It seems possible to me that the people who have left us to be with the Lord can ask God to send us a sign or perhaps a human messenger to let us know that they are with us during the most difficult times of our lives. When we are experiencing emotional distress and sorrow, our friends and relatives who have gone to heaven want us to know that God, the angels, and saints in heaven have not abandoned us. Our departed friends and relatives in heaven want us to know that "the Lord is close to the brokenhearted, (he) saves those whose spirits are crushed." (Psalm 34:19)

On that note, let's take a little music break to listen to the song, "The Eye of The Storm" by Ryan Stevenson.

CHAPTER 14

Our Earth Angels

While Charley was sleeping, I stepped outside to get some fresh air and take a brisk walk. While I was walking, I wished that I had a direct line to Angela and our Lord. I decided to reach out to a close friend of mine who is a nurse. I knew I could count on Lisa to listen and provide words of wisdom and encouragement.

After I was finished explaining my son's medical crisis, Lisa said, "Wow, this is such a difficult situation. I can see why you wanted the brain specialist to speak to your son and address your concerns before the hospital releases him. On the other hand, I could see why Allen thought it was too soon to break the bad news to Charley that he shouldn't wrestle. It's horrible that after everything that has happened, Charley still wants to wrestle!"

I said, "Tell me about it! I feel like taking my head and hitting it against a brick wall a few times to give myself seizures. That way the doctors can place me in a medically induced coma!"

Lisa said, "Oh Francesca! I'm going to drive to Chicago tomorrow to see you and Charley. I also promise you that my family will pray for Charley's complete recovery. We'll pray the rosary for 54 days.

When I hung up the phone with Lisa, I felt a wave of peace come over me. Lisa made good on both of her promises—she visited us at the hospital, and her family said the rosary for 54 days! Their gift of prayer was an extraordinary labor of love! That makes Lisa and her family, first-class angels, and winners at the game of life and love in my book!

Halo Hint

Committing to pray for a friend or family member for a prolonged period is an extraordinary undertaking of a first-class angel.

After Charley was released from the hospital, he went to yet another hospital to receive therapy. He was seventeen years old at the time and was placed in the pediatric unit for victims with brain injuries. Every day, the therapists gently guided him through a series of tests that helped the doctors evaluate his brain function. The therapists didn't want Charley's brain to work too hard for too long. They wanted his brain to begin rebooting itself slowly. Unfortunately, the hospital environment did not help Charley's frame of mind. He became even more depressed while he was trying to recover at the hospital.

I said, "Charley has this hospital provided you with a psychologist for you to speak to?"

Charley said, "Yes, I have spoken to a psychologist, but it is not helping. I feel like ending my life."

I said, "You are going to get through this. All the doctors said your prognosis is good, and you have youth on your side. You have a lot of living left to do. You will recover. Many people are praying for you."

There had been more than one time in my life when I experienced severe depression and a desire to end my life. I regard deep depression, conjoined with the desire to end one's life as being a spiritual attack from the enemy of one's soul. Since my son was experiencing depression and suicidal thoughts, I decided that my son needed a spiritual doctor. I found a priest willing to talk to him and pray with him.

A lot of people were praying for Charley, but I felt the need to recruit an even greater number of prayer warriors to pray for him. It was reassuring to know that there were so many first-class angels who were willing to pray for my son during every stage of his medical crisis.

I also reached out to a healing priest from Chicago, whom I hope will be a canonized saint one day. His name is Father Peter Mary Rookey. Father Peter Rookey prayed for my family members and me many times in his lifetime for physical, spiritual, and emotional healing. Father's assistant promised me that she and Father Rookey would pray for Charley. Father was in his late nineties and was not doing well himself. He passed away a few months later. Father Rookey and his assistant will always be regarded as first-class angels and winners in the game of life and love in my book.

I also called my mother, and I asked her to spend as many days as she could sitting by my son's side while he was in the hospital. No matter how much a person would like to give up on life, no one can go through with such an action when there is a first-class angel standing guard! Many first-class angels stood by Charley's side, but his Grandma Fran kept watch like a first-class archangel!

Halo Hints

When a person is extremely depressed, they need the prayers of many first-class angels. They also need a lot of encouragement and many first-class angels to keep a watchful eye on them.

While Charley was in the hospital, Lily, a former neighbor from my childhood, went out of her way to reach out to me through Facebook and by phone. She told me she was praying very hard for my son, and she understood what we were going through because her daughter had been admitted to a hospital for seizures the year before. I asked Lily if a head injury caused her daughter's seizures.

Lily said, "The doctors never figured out what caused my daughter's seizures. I think they were brought on by stress and a lack of sleep because my daughter had a habit of staying up late at night, texting with her friends."

I said, "I am very sorry to hear about your daughter, and I will pray for her too. I have already been praying for you because I know you have been fighting cancer for quite a while. It's so kind of you to reach out to me and to pray for my son when you are dealing with cancer and your daughter's health problem. Thank you so much."

Advanced Halo Hint

The ability to put aside one's worries and concerns to reach out to someone and pray for their needs is an amazing quality of a first-class angel.

Two years later, I visited Lily at her home. When I inquired about her daughter, she told me the doctors removed a small tumor from her daughter's brain that initially had gone undetected and her daughter was seizure-free. I was happy to hear the wonderful news. We rejoiced together and marveled at God's goodness.

I gave Lily a hug and some blessed oil with the hope that it would help her in her battle against cancer. It was my way of saying thank you to her for reaching out to me and praying for my son during his health crisis. We promised to get together again the next time I came to town.

Lily seemed joyful and full of life on the day that we met in person. To my great sadness, Lily died a couple of months later. When we met, she gave me every reason to believe that she was going to win the battle against cancer. I will always remember Lily for reaching out to me while she was fighting for her life and dealing with her daughter's medical crisis. I know that Lily felt more at peace, knowing that her own daughter's health had been restored. Lily will always be a first-class angel and a winner at the game of life and love in my book.

Sometimes God answers our prayers by healing the people we love of illnesses or removing heavy crosses that are difficult for them to bear. Other times He doesn't, and it is easy to feel as though God has let us down. However, all the high notes and low notes of life are orchestrated by the Lord to draw us into a closer relationship with Him.

I want to end this chapter by asking you to listen to the song called, "The Cure" by Unspoken. This song came on the radio and was playing in the background more than once while I was writing and editing this chapter.

CHAPTER 15

Sunshine Therapy

Though I was not happy that my son was in a hospital, I was grateful to God that it was summer. Having dealt with depression myself on more than one occasion, I knew long days filled with sunshine would make it easier for Charley to overcome depression. Charley's depression and his great need for some fresh air and sunshine were the main reasons we were eager to get him out of the hospital.

While he was still in the hospital, Charley said, "Mom, I am worried that I am not going to be able to remember anything that I learned in high school. I know I used to be smart, but now I feel like I am in special education."

I said, "I have felt like I am in special education my entire life, and I survived. I don't rely only on myself. I pray before I make important decisions. It helps me to make better ones. When I took the board exam to become an esthetician, I felt like I had forgotten everything I learned. I prayed during the test, and I did surprisingly well. You might have to pray too."

After Charley was released from the hospital, his father took him to the Michigan dunes to provide him with a heavy dose of sunshine therapy. Charley felt a burst of energy and the desire to run across the shore. Unfortunately, he was having a hard time walking, let alone running. He fell face forward into the sand. His dad picked Charley up off the ground and told him that if he didn't give up that he would take him on a Hawaiian vacation, and they would go running together on the beaches in Hawaii.

Charley spent the remainder of the summer playing a computerized brain training game called Luminosity as the therapists recommended. He completed every level that Luminosity offered. Charley also spent a lot of time reviewing everything he learned in high school with the help of his sister who provided tutoring. Maria and Tommy ran Charley's lawn maintenance business for him. Even though Charley did not work that summer, he had an income.

I want to thank Maria and Tommy for all you did to help boost Charley's morale that summer. I'd also like to thank Charley's father and stepmother for everything the two of you did to help our son during his darkest hours, and for taking him to the Michigan Dunes and Hawaii for a heavy dose of sunshine therapy. As a token of my thankfulness, I want all of you to know that you are first-class angels and winners at the game of life and love in my book!

Halo Hint

First-class angels know how to lift people's spirits by providing their unique form of sunshine therapy.

I knew sunshine therapy was good for Charley because I have felt the need to self-medicate with sunshine on many occasions. I hope hospital administrators will pay attention to the scientific evidence supporting sunshine and beach therapy because there are some hospitals located close to lakes and oceans that are positioned to provide it.

Gazing at the blue sky and blue water while listening to the rolling waves produces joy and contentment, and it also acts as a natural anti-depressant. It could mean the difference between life and death for some people.

It is my hope and prayer that Chicagoans who are stressed, depressed, or distressed will take advantage of the lakefront and get a dose of sunshine and beach therapy especially during the spring, summer, and early fall. Chicago is meant to be a place of inner healing because it has a beautiful sprawling lakefront that stretches for many miles. When it is cold or gloomy outside, a trip to the indoor atrium made up of tropical plants and trees at Navy Pier is therapeutic as well. Often there is free music entertainment at Navy Pier which serves as another form of therapy.

It is important to keep in mind that our physical, emotional, and spiritual health are intertwined.

Pent-up anger is bad for our emotional well-being and our physical health. It's good to confess when we are angry at God or anybody else. Anger is a deadly sin because it can cause us to do something rash that could lead to our death or the death of someone's reputation. Pent up anger can lead to rage and cause a person to become physically violent. When we confess that we are angry in the presence of a person that possesses a love for God and His commandments, we are much less likely to act on our anger.

James 5:16 in the Bible tells us, "Therefore, confess your sins to one another, pray for one another so that you may be healed." If we are extremely angry, we need to confess our sins of anger to someone who is going to pray for us and with us. It is also prudent to confess our sins of anger to a peaceful person who will try to calm us down rather than talk to somebody who is going to add more fuel to the fire.

The next statement in James 5:16 tells us, "The effective prayer of a righteous man can accomplish much." When we confess our sins to a God-loving person who is willing to pray with us or for us, emotions such as rage, depression, despair, and anxiety have less power over us.

Billions of Catholics and Orthodox Christians throughout the ages, including myself, have experienced a feeling of inner peace and wellbeing by confessing our sins to a priest. If you've never been to the Sacrament of Reconciliation and would like to encounter the healing presence of God found in this amazing sacrament, you can tell the priest that it is your first confession and confess the sins which God places on your heart to confess. Each time you go to confession, it will become a little easier.

Going to confession can be a matter of life or death, especially when a person confesses that they have despaired and are tempted to end their own life. Not only will a priest try to talk a person out of ending their life, but the priest will continue praying for a person after he or she walks out of the confessional. The priest can also direct a person to an organization that offers additional support during a time of crisis.

Confessing our sins to a person who is a representative of God's mercy assists us in making positive changes in our lives. It is good to identify and confess the root of our sin (anger, pride, jealousy, lust, greed) and the sins that we have committed. At times the Holy Spirit will move us to confess our sins of omission, the things we neglected to do that we should have done.

The priest listens and offers advice to help us progress on our spiritual journey. Then he asks us to say an act of sorrow along with some extra prayers after we leave the confessional. Sometimes the priest might ask us to perform an act of kindness.

If people who are depressed, anxious, angry, or distressed made regular use of the Sacrament of Reconciliation, the rate of violence and suicide would decrease, and people would have an easier time overcoming their self-destructive behaviors.

I feel God's love and peace every time I go to confession. The great thing about talking to a priest in the confessional is that what we discuss in a confessional, stays in the confessional. The priest takes a vow of secrecy and cannot reveal to anyone what has been discussed or confessed inside the confessional.

The priest's job is to provide a listening ear, words of comfort, spiritual advice that softens our hearts, and to tell us that our sins are forgiven. The Sacrament of Reconciliation is truly the greatest form of therapy that exists on the planet!

Most Catholic Churches provide the Sacrament of Reconciliation right before Mass on Saturday evenings between 3:00 and 4:30. To find out when confession and Masses are taking place at any Catholic Church near you, you can get an app called MassTimes.

Priests are also available to hear confessions at many hospitals and nursing homes. Many major cities have churches that provide the Sacrament of Reconciliation every day.

It is good to form the habit of going to the Sacrament of Reconciliation on a regular basis. I prefer to go to confession once a month. Another good option is to go four times a year at the beginning of each season, or two times a year before Christmas and Easter.

A simple acknowledgment of our faults and a gentle nudge from the priest telling us to do better is one of the easiest ways to improve our spiritual and mental health, which in turn boosts our physical health, and restores our sense of worth.

It feels good to know that God loves us and forgives us even when we've made big mistakes, and it is as though we have fallen face-first into the sand. Just like my son Charley, we need to experience a loving father's hand reaching out to pick us up off the ground. We also need a loving father telling us that we need to try to do our best to get better. We can have that type of experience as often as we need it in the Sacrament of Reconciliation.

Halo Hints

God's presence and His healing power are present in nature and the Sacrament of Reconciliation.

Confession of our sins is a great way to buff out the dents in our halos and adjust our wings so that we can soar to a higher realm of love!

On that note, let's take a music break to listen to the song, "Healing Begins" with Tenth Avenue North.

CHAPTER 16

Lifting Minds & Heart Through Music & the Arts

When I was a young mother, I was one of the typical moms from the 1990s who went out and purchased a CD called Baby Maestro to play for my children. I read somewhere that playing classical music could increase a child's intelligence. My children turned out to be a lot smarter than I am as was indicated by their grade point averages, their ACT scores—and their ability to win arguments!

On my train ride home from the hospital, I found myself wondering—where was the music therapy for the children, especially the children recovering from brain injuries? That's when the latent Julie Andrews that has been locked up inside of my heart since childhood awakened and began feeling a strong, uncontrollable desire to give the gift of music to children at children's hospitals!

Words can't express how much I would love to sing to children at children's hospitals. Unfortunately, my singing voice is more like that of Julie Andrews' after she developed nodules on her vocal chords. Even if I could carry a tune, it's not like I can *pop in* on the children in hospital wards as though I am another Mary Poppins and begin singing, due to issues surrounding security.

I wish life was a musical, and we all could spontaneously burst into a song to more fully express what we are thinking and feeling. I think that is how we are going to speak to God, the angels, and to each other when we get to heaven.

When God places something on my heart, I must do something to answer His call even if it is only something small. A few years after my son was released from the hospital, I decided to give a karaoke machine to one of my friends who has a beautiful singing voice, so she could sing to and with the children in a preschool where she teaches.

I also decided to call some hospitals while I was visiting my family in Chicago to find out if any music therapists would be interested in providing a Christmas-Karaoke sing-along with me to the children. Even though I do not have a beautiful singing voice, I thought it would be nice to sing "Jingle Bells" and "Santa Claus is Coming to Town" with the children.

After speaking to several answering machines, I gave up on my wish to go on a Christmas-karaoke mission trip.

After the Christmas holiday, one music therapist from Lurie Children's Hospital in Chicago returned my phone call. I was so happy to hear back because I had worked down the street from the hospital many years before.

The therapist said, "I'm sorry I didn't get back to you before the holiday. I was out of town. We would love to receive a karaoke machine as a donation. It could be used by the children who are waiting for a heart transplant to help alleviate their boredom."

I said, "I'm so happy to hear that! I would love to come in and sing with you and the children, but I am no longer in Chicago. I was visiting family over the holidays, but I am back in Louisiana. I will be more than happy to send a karaoke machine through the mail for you to use with the children."

She said, "We look forward to receiving it."

I said, "My son had a long hospital stay in Chicago, and he never received music therapy. He kept getting more depressed the longer he stayed in the hospital. I still do not understand why he never received music therapy. Is there a shortage of music therapists?"

She said, "I'm sorry to hear that your son did not receive any music therapy. Most hospitals have one or two music therapists on staff, and music therapy can be made available to patients upon request."

I said, "I didn't realize that I had to put in a request. Since nobody offered music therapy to my son, I assumed that the hospital did not offer it."

She said, "Even though your son did not stay here, I will provide our hospital with your feedback."

After scoring a winning point with Lurie Hospital, I donated a karaoke machine to Saint Jude Children's Research Hospital in Memphis, Tennessee.

I do not know how often the children's hospitals utilize the karaoke machines. I hope karaoke will boost the children 's morale and bring them joy during a difficult time in their lives.

While writing this chapter, I learned that the under-pinnings of music therapy began during World War I and World War II, when many groups of musicians volunteered to provide entertainment to soldiers who were suffering from emotional and physical trauma. It was a huge volunteer effort that took place across the country during the post-war era, as musicians (both professional and amateur) provided entertainment to the soldiers at veteran's hospitals. The doctors who witnessed this happening could not help but notice that music entertainment elevated the soldiers' moods and accelerated the rate of recovery.

To get some idea of what that might have been like for the soldiers, I ask you to look up one of "Bob Hope Entertains The Troops" videos on YouTube.

Bob Hope and several other entertainers put on musical and comedy performances for numerous soldiers during more than one war. They also visited wounded soldiers in makeshift hospitals. This part of American history speaks volumes about the importance of volunteerism.

After the World War I and II, hospital administrators decided that college training was necessary for musicians to interact with patients. However, preapproved musicians and vocalists can also work with therapists at hospitals.

Musicians on Call (MOC)

If by chance you are interested in working as a volunteer song artist or musician at a hospital, you can do so in conjunction with a wonderful nonprofit organization called "Musicians on Call" or "MOC." According to its website, MOC delivers live, in-room performances to patients with the help of volunteers. Since 1999, MOC volunteer musicians have performed for over 600,000 patients and their families. Bedside performances currently take place in twenty cities throughout the United States. MOC is looking for advocates to bring volunteer musicians to more hospitals. It also needs volunteer guides to work with volunteer musicians. More information about MOC can be found at musiciansoncall.org.

Halo Hint

Sharing one's gifts and talents with others and bringing people joy during a difficult time in their lives is a beautiful quality of a first-class angel.

The loss of some of my dearest friends to cancer, a cousin who spent the last five years of his life trying to recover from a stroke, and my son's medical crisis has awakened a desire in me to lift minds and hearts through music and the arts. However, I can only fly to a higher realm of love by joining wings and voices with other first-class angels.

CHAPTER 17

Meddling with Love

Charley called me about a month after he left the hospital. He said, "Mom, I have decided that I am going to find a doctor that will provide a release for me to wrestle. I have also decided that I don't want you to be involved in the decisions concerning my health care. I appreciate your love and support, but you're too overly protective."

That's when I called on the assistance of other first-class angels for backup support. First, I called my brother John and asked him if he and his wife, Kathy, were in the mood for company, knowing already that family was always welcome. Then I called my brother Ray and asked him to drive Charley to John's house on Lake Keowee, a beautiful place in South Carolina. Then I got on my computer and booked a flight for myself to fly to South Carolina for a family intervention.

Within the first two days of being at Lake Keowee, my brother John lined up a job for Charley at one of the largest landscaping businesses in the Clemson area. The owner told Charley that he would teach him everything about the business. Charley seemed interested in working for the gentlemen, and I couldn't have been happier.

Halo Hint

Going to bat for someone is an admirable quality of a first-class angel.

Next, we took Charley on a tour of Clemson University. John pointed out that the girls at Clemson University out-numbered the guys four to one, knowing that Charley's heart was still on the mend from his breakup with his high school sweetheart. While touring the beautiful campus on a bright sunshiny day, it seemed as though Charley was warming up to the idea of attending Clemson University. Unfortunately, a cold front came through right after Charley checked out Clemson's website on his smartphone and learned that Clemson did not have a wrestling team.

There were three reasons why I wanted Charley to attend Clemson University. First, I knew that some-day I would migrate to the southeastern region of the United States, and I wanted all my first-class angels to migrate there before I arrived there. Secondly, I knew Clemson was an excellent school that did not offer wrestling. Lastly, I wanted my son to attend a college that was close to family, in case of an emergency.

I was disappointed that Charley did not want to attend Clemson University, but I thought the trip was not a waste of anybody's time. It's always nice to visit my brother and his family. The weather was beautiful, and it provided Charley with another dose of sunshine therapy. I'm sure Charley also realized that he has a loving family who is more than willing to go the distance for him and that we had his best interests at heart.

After I got home from South Carolina, I called another first-class angel whom I hoped would be able to persuade Charley to fly in another direction. That first-class angel was Charley's older sister.

Maria said, "Charley should attend Life University with me in Atlanta. Life has a wrestling team and good undergraduate programs. Even if he ends up wrestling, I will do my best to keep an eye on him."

I said, "I wish there were a way to convince Charley to give up wrestling!"

Maria said, "If Charley goes to Life University, he will associate with many chiropractors and students who are health conscious. He might decide to focus on his health and give up wrestling."

I said, "It sounds like a good game plan, Maria."

Before we hung up the phone, Maria promised that she would call her brother and talk to him about attending Life University.

Charley responded by saying, "I don't want to give up my dream to attend Northwestern University. The wrestling coaches are on standby waiting to find out if I will be released to wrestle."

Two weeks later, I learned that Charley was unable to obtain the financing that he needed to attend Northwestern University. Instead of going to a university, Charley took a couple of humanities classes at a junior college. It saddened me that my son had to endure such great disappointment. However, I viewed it as being a blessing in disguise. The brain specialist I spoke to a few months before told me that it would be good for Charley to attend a junior college and take things slow. I felt like I could breathe a little easier.

Unfortunately, it was a short breather. A couple of months later, Charley informed me that he found a neurologist that released him to train for wrestling. He had just turned eighteen and was an adult in the eyes of the law.

I cannot speak for other people, but it is easier for me to surrender my battles to the Lord when I have no other option. 2 Chronicles 20:15 reminds me/us, "the battle is not yours, (mine, or ours) but God's." When our hands are tied, we should know with greater clarity that the battle belongs to the Lord.

If God is fighting our battles and our children's battles while our hands are tied, the only thing we can do is stand back and watch God fight for us as we sing a battle cry to the Lord. There are some excellent Christian song artists available to help us play our part.

On that note, let's take a music break to listen to (and sing) the song, "Surrounded – Fight My Battles" by Michael W. Smith

CHAPTER 18

Baby Bird Flies from the Nest

Charley attended an excellent university in the Midwest the following year which provided him with an academic and a wrestling scholarship. He complained more than once that academics was a struggle for him, but he did well by maintaining a 3.0-grade point average. I was very proud of him, as were all his family members.

I can't say how well Charley did in wrestling. I never attended his wrestling meets. I did not want to give him the impression that I was on board with it.

Before his official freshmen year in college, I showed up to one of his practices and introduced myself to the head coach as the parent that did not approve of my son wrestling.

While Charley was giving me a tour of the campus, he saw his assistant coach riding his bike and pointed him out to me. Then Charley said, "My assistant coach is an epileptic."

I said, "Charley, why do you think the assistant coach has seizures?"

Charley did not answer my question. Instead, he informed me that the head coach granted Charley permission to be on the wrestling team with the stipulation that if he had any seizures that he would let the coach know.

A few months later, the head coach found out that Charley had a seizure that he tried to keep hidden. The head coach quickly dismissed Charley from the wrestling team.

I am grateful to the head coach for playing his part to keep my son honest. I also believe the coach was concerned about my son's long-term brain health. From my standpoint, the head coach was a first-class angel and a winner at the game of life and love!

Halo Hint

There are times when a first-class angel must be willing to provide tough love.

About a week later Charley announced on Facebook that it was the end of his wrestling career. Many people offered him their condolences while I thanked God for answering my prayer. Once again, I felt like I could breathe easier. Once again it was a short breather. Less than a month later, Charley found another wrestling coach at another college who had prior experience coaching another wrestler who had seizures. He welcomed Charley onto his team.

I asked Charley, "Why do you think we are seeing a pattern of seizures among wrestlers?"

Charley said, "The wrestler developed seizures as a child."

Charley knew that I suspected that he was trying to pull the wool over my eyes. He then assured me that he was going to be on a third-division wrestling team, and it was not going to be as intense as wrestling on a first-division wrestling team.

I know that God heard my prayers, but I also know that God listened to Charley's prayers. God knew the desires of his heart and my heart. Perhaps wrestling on the third-division team was God's way of providing a compromise to Charley and me.

I went one entire wrestling season without meddling. However, as soon as an opportunity presented itself, I let the new coach know that I was very concerned about my son's brain health. This time I was fully prepared to have an honest, open discussion with the wrestling coach in the presence of my son about my son's health issues. So, I took Charley and his wrestling coach out for dinner at a steakhouse, and the three of us had a long discussion.

I don't know exactly how it happened, but somehow the two of them buttered me up, and sweet talked me into believing, at least temporarily, that there was no need for me to be concerned. Perhaps it was that my mind needed to take a short vacation from worry and concern. Perhaps it was that Charley's coach assured me that he was watching out for Charley as though was his own brother. Perhaps it was that the wrestling coach was half-Irish and half-Italian, and I felt a measure of affinity with him.

I'm still not happy that Charley figured out a way to wrestle at the college level, but I thank God for giving Charley another brother from an Italian mother and an Irish father.

More importantly, I got the feeling that the wrestling coach is humble, kind, and tender-hearted. That makes him a first-class angel and winner at the game of life and love in my book.

Halo Hint

Being humble, kind, tender-hearted, and easy to talk to are some of the most important qualities of a first-class angel.

Possessing those qualities are so important that a country song artist wrote a song about them. The person who wrote the song happens to be a mother of five children. Her name is Lori McKenna. Thank you, Lori, for writing a beautiful song that has touched my heart and the hearts of my children.

Let's take a little music break to listen to Lori sing, "Humble and Kind."

I also thank God for giving Charley a college sweetheart who is as beautiful on the inside as she is on the outside. She enjoys watching Charley wrestle and has gained favor with both of us by learning how to make Italian meatballs for him. Thus far, she has remained by Charley's side even though she is aware of his health issues. She's a good woman with a brave heart. That makes her a first-class angel and winner at the game of life and love in my book.

Halo Hint

Possessing a brave heart and remaining by somebody's side in the face of adversity are outstanding qualities of a first-class angel.

I am grateful to God that He has assigned two guardian angels in human form to keep a watchful eye on my son in the absence of his family members. To express my gratitude to those two first-class angels, I invited them to my house to spend the Easter holiday with my family. We made homemade pizza, got to know each other better, and made a great memory.

Halo Hint

When we feel as though our faith is being put to the test, it is important for first-class angels to continue enjoying life to the fullest.

On that note let's take a little music break to listen to John Finch sing "Walk by Faith."

CHAPTER 19

How to Befriend First-Class Angels

In the first chapter of this book, I shared a **halo hint** that makes it easier for us to operate as first-class angels. I want to share it with you once again.

Halo Hint

It is important to form friendships, partnerships, and alliances with other first-class angels and minimize the time that we spend with people who drag us down.

In the first chapter, I also provided you with a list of qualities that first-class angels possess so that you can easily identify them. As a review, I would like to provide the list once again.

- **First-class angels strive to be loving and tender-hearted.**

- **First-class angels strive to be humble and kind.**

- **First-class angels do not play mind games.**

- **First-class angels tread lightly on people's emotions.**

- **First-class angels strive to be at peace with themselves and other people.**

- **First-class angels bring out the best in others.**

- **First-class angels defend the honor of others.**

- **First-class angels do not dwell on the faults of others and are inclined to make light of people's faults.**

- **First-class angels inspire others to be first-class angels through their loving example.**

Some of the easiest ways to find other first-class angels and form friendships with them are to become an active member of a church or do some volunteer work with members from your church or community. Another way to find other first-class angels is to pray that God will bring people who operate as first-class angels into your life. After you pray, you must trust that God answered your prayer and be "a love paparazzi" who is on the lookout for first-class angels who spread love and do good everywhere.

Amazing Blessings

Some first-class angels in my church plan and go on pilgrimages to nurture their relationship with the Lord. Pilgrimages are planned at least once a year at Saint Jude Church in Benton, Louisiana. More than one group of people from my church has traveled to the Holy Land and promised to pray for the parishioners.

Our associate pastor, Father Jerry Daigle, went to the Holy Land in March of 2017 and brought back small holy cards which he touched to the ground on Calvary, where Jesus died and to the sepulcher from which Jesus rose again. I am grateful and honored to have received one of the holy cards. I keep it tucked in a collage that contains photos of my five children, three stepchildren, Joe and me.

Father Jerry prayed very hard for the special intentions of our church community while he was in the Holy Land. That makes our associate pastor a first-class angel and winner in the game of life and love in my book!

Some of my friends from Saint Jude Catholic Church visited Fatima and Lourdes in September of 2017. Fatima is in Portugal. Lourdes is in France. Fatima and Lourdes are two holy places where the Blessed Mother has appeared and has given the world important messages from our Lord.

At my request, my friends, Susan and Jake, kept Charley and a close friend of our family in their prayers in a special way during their pilgrimage. When my friend Susan came back from her pilgrimage, she told me that she and her husband Jake truly carried my intentions in their hearts while they visited many holy sites in Europe. That makes Susan and Jake first-class angels and winners at the game of life and love in my book!

Let's Do Lunch!

I met Susan at a ladies' luncheon called, "Magnificat." Magnificat is a Catholic ladies' group that meets for lunch, prayer, worship, and fellowship four times a year. I have met many other first-class angels at our Magnificat luncheons. Magnificat originated in New Orleans, but it also has chapters throughout the United States and other countries. To find a Magnificat chapter near you or to start up a Magnificat chapter in your neck of the woods, you can send an email to magnificatcst@aol.com or call (504) 828-MARY (6279) to request information.

The Wine & Rosary Party

As a writer, I spend too much time sitting in front of my computer. One way that I force myself to be more social is by throwing wine and rosary parties. No matter how few or how many people show up, it is always a blessing to eat, drink wine, socialize, and pray the rosary with my spiritual family. I am happy to say that my wine and rosary parties are growing in popularity among males and females, and people of all ages!

People often ask, why do Catholics pray to Mary? We ask Mother Mary to pray for us and with us because we know that if Mother Mary was able to get Jesus to perform His first public miracle, by turning water into wine at a wedding when the wine ran out that she could also get Jesus to perform other miracles for us.

I enjoy having wine and rosary parties because Jesus performed His first miracle by changing water into wine at His mother's request while they were at a wedding. One of my favorite decades of the rosary is "The Wedding at Cana." I believe that drinking wine and praying the rosary is a perfect marriage!

Not only is Mary the mother of Jesus, but she is the spouse of the Holy Spirit because she conceived Jesus by the power of the Holy Spirit. Like all Christians, she is an adopted child of God the Father. When we pray the rosary, the Blessed Mother helps us to draw closer to all three persons of the Holy Trinity as we meditate on the life, death, and resurrection of Jesus Christ.

I love partnering in prayer with Mother Mary because she has more clout with all three persons of the Holy Trinity than all the people on Earth and all the angels and saints in heaven put together. Mary has a compassionate heart, and her words spoken on our behalf pull mightily on God's heartstrings.

To get a better idea of how to pray the rosary, you can go to www.comepraytherosary.org. Not only will this website teach you how to pray the prayers and meditate on the twenty mysteries of the rosary, but it will also take you on a visual pilgrimage to places in the Holy Land where Jesus was born, preached, healed people, died, rose from the dead, and ascended into heaven.

Father John Bosco, the first priest I spoke to when Charley went into the hospital years ago, told me to consecrate Charley to the Blessed Mother. Consecrating ourselves and our children to Mother Mary is a special way of entrusting ourselves and our children to her motherly care.

There are many ways to consecrate our children and ourselves to Mother Mary. One of the simplest ways to do it is simply by saying, "Mary, Mother of Jesus, please be a mother to (my children and) me."

I love that Mother Mary is my mother and my friend. I hope and pray that all my children will recognize the importance of consecrating themselves and their children to Mother Mary so that she can be that much more of a mother and friend to them. If you have not done so, I hope and pray that you will consecrate yourself to Mother Mary. After you do, I hope you will develop a love for the rosary and invite some of your friends to your home to celebrate by having a wine and rosary party!

Praying the rosary is a great way to consecrate our country to The Blessed Mother's care, especially when we have the intention of saying one Hail Mary for every state. There are fifty main beads on the rosary. It is as though the rosary was designed for the United States. Mother Mary is also the Patroness of the United States.

On that note, let's take a music break to prayerfully listen to the song "Ave Maria" sung by Celine Dion.

CHAPTER 20

To Wear a Helmet or Not Wear a Helmet?

Two years after my son was released from the hospital, I was at a Clemson football game with my brother John and his family. John was wearing a vintage leather football helmet. He looked goofy, but I like goofy at times. I found myself wondering if a leather helmet would be beneficial for wrestlers to wear in that it covers much of the skull, the forehead, and the ears.

A few weeks later, I told Charley that I wanted to find a good helmet for wrestlers. I hoped that a helmet that has some padding on the forehead might provide a wide enough gap to protect the eyes when two wrestlers inadvertently head-butt each other.

I looked further into helmets and learned that some companies in Europe are creating soft-shell helmets for skiers, bicyclists, and motorcyclists. I thought that was interesting because they are so vulnerable to high-speed, high-impact accidents. I wondered if the European companies did studies with crash test dummies to determine how effectively a softshell helmet would protect the skull in the event of a serious accident.

After watching the movie, *Concussion*, I was uncertain if wearing any helmet would protect the brain. By shaking a clear jar that contained water and a round object, Dr. Bennet Omalu (played by Will Smith) demonstrated how the brain could crash into the inside of the skull when it experiences trauma. He also pointed out in the movie that God did not provide the brain with an internal shock-absorber.

After I watched the movie several times, I realized that the jar was filled only about halfway with water. Moreover, the ratio of water to the round object inside the jar and the ratio of water to the brain inside a skull did not appear to be the correct ratio. I had a difficult time imagining the brain crashing into the inner wall of the skull when the head experiences trauma.

One day I was driving down the road with a cake sitting right beside me on the passenger seat. I hit the brakes a little too forcefully when coming to a stop. The cake slid off the seat onto the floor. Sure enough, the cake crashed into the inner wall of the container. In this case, the only thing that stood between the cake and the inner wall of the container was airspace and the icing on the cake. Only the icing on the cake got damaged, not the cake itself.

I thanked God for the visual lesson. However, I still wanted to try to determine if a soft-shell helmet would offer wrestlers any form of protection.

About two weeks later, out of the blue, I decided to experiment by shaking three eggs about thirty times each. As I was shaking the eggs, it truly felt as though the eggs were scrambling inside of their shells. When I cracked open the eggs, I was surprised to see that the yolks were not broken. During my initial inspection, the egg white seemed to have done a good job of preventing the yolk from crashing into the inner wall of the eggshell. Upon closer inspection, I noticed that each egg yolk seemed to be a little flatter and more swollen than a normal yolk. There was also an indentation or slight crater inside two of the three yolks.

Then I took three unshaken eggs and cracked them open into three bowls. All three unshaken eggs had rounder yolks, and there was no crater-like indention in the yolks. This experiment caused me to wonder if an athlete's brain could eventually collapse inside their skull if their brain had been traumatized many times over the course of their career.

An observation that anybody could make on their own to test the functionality of a light-weight, soft-shell helmet is to look inside a carton of eggs before purchasing them from the market. Each pocket inside the carton is like a little, softshell helmet for an egg. When we open the carton before purchasing them, there are times when none of the eggs are broken. Other times, we will find one or two broken eggs. Based on this observation, we could safely assume that a light-weight, soft-shell helmet would provide the cranium with partial protection by lessening the risk of skull fractures. That by itself is an important function of a helmet.

The following week, I found an unopened jar of large pickles inside my pantry. The pickles were fully submerged in pickle juice. When I shook the jar of pickles several times, the pickles crashed into the inside wall of the jar. However, I was happy to see that the pickles remained unharmed. After giving it more thought, I realized that a human brain is not as delicate as egg yolk, but not as durable as a pickle.

A pickle has one and possibly two advantages over the human brain. A pickle has an outer casing to protect the innards of the pickle. Moreover, the pickle is rubbery. That is why the pickles bounced off the inside wall of the jar and remained unharmed.

Unfortunately, I have never held a human brain in my hand. I did not know the texture of the brain. I did not know if the brain has a membrane to encase the various lobes of the brain. Even an egg yolk has a membrane, though very thin. Much was left to my imagination.

I read this chapter to my neighbor. Kelly thought it was very interesting. I told her that we should go to the sushi restaurant located on the Louisiana Boardwalk and order the monkey brain from the menu; hoping that there might be some similarity between a monkey brain and a human brain. Kelly agreed that we needed to go to the restaurant to check it out.

The next day when Kelly was visiting, I asked her to call the restaurant ahead of time to make sure that we would be able to get our hands on some raw monkey brain. The person who answered the phone said it would not be a problem, and it would cost about ten dollars. I told Kelly to tell them that I needed a large portion of monkey brain and not to chop it up, because I needed to use it for my son's science experiment. Then the person on the phone retracted their statement and said it would be a problem because they never serve monkey brain raw, and that it was made up of avocado, crab meat, tuna, and cream cheese. Apparently, monkey brain in sushi restaurants is not made with real monkey brain. It is a tongue-in-cheek name given to sushi.

This is what I get for acting like Curious George!

Do Not Try This Experiment!

Still curious, I decided to be my own crash test dummy. I wagged my head back and forth, swiftly several times (about twelve times, from side to side).

I could not feel any fluid shaking around inside my skull. I did not feel as though I was scrambling my brains like I did when I shook the eggs inside their shells. However, I could feel my brain bouncing around inside my skull. I could not tell how much fluid surrounded my brain or the size of my brain by shaking my head. All I can tell you is that I did not feel good after I wagged my head back and forth about twelve times. It made me feel dizzy and slightly nauseous. It gave me a headache. It also made me feel as though I ought to take a nap.

Instead of taking a nap, I finished writing about my observations and loaded my dishwasher. Then I checked my pupils in the mirror to make sure that they were not dilated. They were fine. I went to sleep for about three hours. Even after I woke up from my nap, I felt like I had brain fog for the remainder of the evening. For the next several weeks, I woke up with headaches in the morning. Under normal circumstances, I rarely get headaches.

I have never had a concussion that I can recall. However, I am convinced that I experienced brain trauma when I wagged my head back and forth several times. I could place a helmet on my head and try wagging my head again, but already think I would end up with the same results or I might experience symptoms that are worse.

Nobody, I repeat nobody, should try wagging or shaking their head or someone else's head in that it could cause trauma to the brain.

I just wanted to find out for myself if wearing a helmet would help any of my sons in the event of a head injury. Sometimes my sons go on long bike rides, halfway across the country with my brother Ray. I've come to realize that it is important for parents to learn as much as we can about helmets.

I was more perplexed about the pros and cons of wearing a helmet after I volunteered to be my own crash test dummy. Nonetheless, I continued to hold onto hope that a soft-shell helmet would offer athletes at least some protection.

I can't help but notice that God was kind enough to give oranges, lemons, and limes a lightweight, rubbery, soft-shell helmet as a form of protection. I still feel a great need to offer similar protection to my sons.

As I stated before, I truly did not want Charley wrestling after he was released from the hospital. Retiring from wrestling is the best way to protect his brain from injuries. If he feels the need to wrestle or go on a long bike ride, I feel the need to offer him some protection by purchasing a good helmet for him to wear.

Even though I could not come up with any scientific proof, something inside of me told me that Charley should wear a light-weight, soft-shell helmet that covers his head, forehead, and ears as opposed to wearing headgear that only covers his ears while he wrestles.

I am not a doctor, scientist, or an engineer. I am only a mom that is trying to do her best to make a good judgment call on behalf of my son. I've been around long enough to know that when it comes to scientific research that doctors and scientists do not always arrive at the same conclusions. There are times when they provide us with conflicting information and misinformation. Doctors are not infallible. Sometimes they tell us one thing, and years later, they tell us something that is entirely different.

For example, while I was growing up, doctors told us that eggs could increase our cholesterol levels. Now doctors are saying eggs do not increase our cholesterol levels, and that they are good for us.

My mother believed that her family should continue eating eggs while I was growing up. She believed eggs were good for us despite what the doctors told us. My mother had good instincts. I have learned that I must trust my instincts too.

Today everyone believes (including doctors) that it is prudent for a person or a child to wear a helmet when riding a bike. If it is prudent to wear a helmet when riding a bike, wouldn't it be prudent to wear a helmet when wrestling, playing soccer, or any sport where athletes can inadvertently collide and experience head-to-head injuries?

And yet, an article in highschoolsports.al.com dated April 29, 2016, says that the use of helmets in soccer is likely to do more harm than good. According to the article, one of the reasons doctors do not want soccer players to wear helmets is because they are concerned that the weight of a helmet will turn the soccer player into a bobblehead, and it would increase the likelihood of whiplash when a soccer player falls to the ground.

I agree that wearing a helmet will not prevent whiplash. I could also see how doctors might be concerned that wearing a helmet could turn soccer players into bobbleheads, causing a worse case of whiplash. Have the doctors considered the use of a light-weight, soft-shell helmet, so soccer players do not turn into bobbleheads?

Perhaps, the main reason European companies are creating softshell helmets for motorcyclists, bicyclists, and skiers is to prevent them from turning into bobbleheads. Who should we trust?

The article in highschoolsports.al.com also stated that head-to-head and elbow-to-head injuries are the most serious types of injuries for soccer players. If they are the most serious types of injuries, don't we need to offer some form of protection?

I decided to perform a small test to discover the potential impact of sub-concussive blows to the brain by taking a small hammer and striking my knee cap about five times. Striking my knee with a small hammer five times could be described as pain at the level of 2.5 on a scale of one to five, with five being the worst. Then I took a terry cloth headband and wrapped it around the same knee and performed the same test. I could feel the hammer striking my knee just as before, but my level of pain dropped. I felt no pain.

If you have ever hit your elbow against a hard surface very hard, you might have felt a great deal of unexpected pain. Moreover, you might have felt the pain that traveled up or down your arm. If you hit a hard surface with your elbow, with the same amount of force, while wearing padding on your elbow, you would feel less pain and possibly no pain at all.

It is important to note **that it is the impact of the blow that causes the pain** that you feel in your elbow when you hit it against a hard surface, as well as **the traveling pain** that you sometimes feel in your arm when you hit your elbow against a hard surface.

It is also important to note that **nerve damage could travel from one side of the brain to the other side of the brain. Nerve damage could also take place in the center of the brain or on a diagonal. Much is dependent on the angle and impact of the blow.** At least that is what I was told by a brain specialist in Chicago about a week after my son came out of the medically induced coma.

If we can prevent pain from traveling by wearing padding, shouldn't we be able to prevent or at least hinder nerve damage from traveling across the brain by wearing a padded helmet as well?

I believe it is possible to lessen the impact of a blow, in an elbow-to-head injury or a head-to-head injury, simply by allowing soccer players and other athletes to wear a light-weight, soft-shell helmet with the hope that it would prevent or at least hinder nerve damage from traveling across the brain.

I ask parents to talk to a doctor who possesses an interest in protecting athletes from brain injuries. Ask him or her to read this chapter. Then I ask you to ask him or her whether the following statement is **true or false**:

"A lightweight, soft-shell helmet cannot offer any guarantees that it will prevent brain damage, but it can offer us some assurance that it will lessen the impact of a blow. By lessening the impact of the blow, we can hope to lessen the amount of brain damage that might occur."

It has been a while since my children have played soccer, but there are protective headgear and halos available for soccer players that can be found online. I saw a halo with a pony-tail opening for girls that is adorable. Soccer players can also wear elbow pads to lessen the impact of an elbow-to-head injury. More than one source told me that wearing a mouth guard can lessen the impact of a blow to the brain as well. I looked it up on the internet and found evidence to support two doctors' claims.

After you talk to a doctor, you can decide whether you would like to purchase a soft-shell helmet, halo headgear, elbow pads, and a mouth guard for your child. After you have made your decision, you can discuss it with parents and coaches.

On that note, let's take a music break to listen to the songs called, "Brain Song for Kids" found on YouTube.

CHAPTER 21

The Helmet-Maker

Just before the 2017-2018 wrestling season, I found a helmet online which is designed with wrestlers in mind. It's called the Mercado. The Mercado is constructed with a patent-pending blend of elastomeric polymer and viscoelastic foam materials. Because of its elasticity, the Mercado has been constructed to conform to an athlete's head. It has some open airways, so the wrestler's head does not overheat. It is stylish, and it looks like something a warrior would wear.

I watched a video of Mario Mercado wrestling while wearing the Mercado. It remained in place even when his opponent was swatting at his forehead. In another video, there were two young girls engaged in kickboxing while wearing the Mercado. I wasn't put off by their gender because Charley grew up with a female Olympian wrestler.

I called the BATS-TOI Corporation to purchase the Mercado for my sons. Mario Mercado Jr. answered the phone. He informed me that the Mercado had already been sold out, and I would not be able to get the helmets for at least a month. With every intention of hiding my disappointment, I congratulated Mario on the success of the Mercado and thanked him for creating it. The gratitude which I expressed to Mario Mercado was meant to have been not only on behalf of my son but for other wrestlers.

I was happy to learn that Mario had been working with engineers and scientists from a highly reputable institution here in the United States as well as a manufacturer in Italy to create a soft-shell helmet for wrestlers long before the idea entered my mind.

I feel as though I can say with confidence that "the Lord understands my thoughts from afar, even before a word is on my tongue, the Lord knows it all." (Psalm 139:2 and 4)

I am grateful to God that Mario Mercado Jr. and his team of scientists and engineers have taken on a mission to create a helmet for wrestlers. Mario has used his resources to create the helmet and has also helped many scientists and engineers put their brains to good use. That makes Mario Mercado Jr. a first-class angel and a winner at the game of life and love in my book!

Halo Hint

Going to great lengths to protect an athlete's brain is a heroic undertaking of a first-class angel.

On that note, let's take a music break to listen to the song, "Twinkle, Twinkle Brain of Mine" that can be found on the internet.

CHAPTER 22

Crossed Signals

When my son Charley was a little boy, I dressed him up as Saint Michael, the archangel, for Halloween. I bought a knight costume for him from a Christian store that had a plastic helmet, a breastplate with a cross on it, and a sword. The breastplate covered up most of his little body. His beautiful blond curls were sticking out of his helmet. He ended up looking more like a cherub than Saint Michael, the archangel.

Charley loved his costume, and he took his job as Saint Michael, the archangel, very seriously. As Divine Providence orchestrated it, Charley spotted a lady dressed up as a devil, passing out candy on her front porch. He ran up to the devil as fast as his little legs would take him and thrust his sword at her throat. He stopped just short of making any physical contact. Charley caught the devil off guard and gave her quite a scare. It was the only time in my entire life that I felt the need to apologize to the devil for the behavior of one of my little holy terrors!

One of the reasons my children were highly spirited even as young children was because I allowed them to watch the movie, *Joan of Arc*, many times when they were young. It was one of our favorite family movies. As we watched the movie, I believed that it was teaching my children some important spiritual lessons.

I wanted my children to grow up to be strong, emotionally and spiritually, just like Saint Joan of Arc. If it were necessary, I wanted (and still want) them to be willing to die for their faith. I also gravitated to the movie, *Joan of Arc*, because I loved the way Charlotte Church sang "Panis Angelicus" (Bread of Angels) when the French soldiers went into battle.

My children were very young when they watched the movie, *Joan of Arc*, and did not understand that the song, "Panis Angelicus," was meant to convey the message that when we go into battle, we need to obtain strength from the Bread of Angels, which is a metaphor for Holy Communion.

Charley, more than my other children, seemed to understand the importance of Holy Communion because he used to pretend that he was a priest and would attempt to consecrate bread and grape juice at our kitchen table when he was in preschool.

When he was a little boy, he also could not wait to make his First Holy Communion. One Sunday morning Charley got dressed in his best suit, shirt, and tie. He looked quite dapper. Then he announced that he was going to make his First Holy Communion. I thought, *Awe, isn't he adorable. He thinks that he's going to make his First Holy Communion today*. During the busyness of the morning, I never took the time to explain to Charley that he needed to wait a little longer before he could make his First Holy Communion.

When it was time for Holy Communion, Charley followed me up to the altar. I was deep in prayer and had forgotten that Charley had informed me earlier that morning that he was going to make his First Holy Communion. No sooner I received Holy Communion; I heard Charley scream, "I got one!" Everybody in the church started laughing out loud, except for the priest who seemed displeased with my son's lack of reverence. I turned around, and saw Charley's hands still outstretched, with a Holy Communion host sitting in the palm of his little hand. Charley's face was beaming with happiness and pride. Before he could place the Eucharist in his mouth, I lifted the Holy Communion host out of his palm and gave the Eucharist back to the priest.

Perhaps, I should have allowed Charley to receive his First Holy Communion that day. Looking back, I truly believe that his heart was more than ready to receive Jesus in Holy Communion and that he had been ready for a long time.

I hope you will take a little walk down memory lane with me by listening to Charlotte Church sing "Panis Angelicus (Live)." This version of Panis Angelicus is my favorite. Make sure you type in Charlotte Church's name and the word "Live" when looking it up.

Then There Was Rocky

After my children's father and I went through a divorce, my children got to witness the beauty of the Sacrament of Marriage while watching the movie, *Rocky*.

We witnessed Rocky pray with great fervor for his wife when she went into a coma after giving birth to their son. We witnessed how Rocky would not leave Adrienne's side in the hospital. We witnessed a miracle when Adrienne woke up from the coma.

We also witnessed Rocky and Adrienne love each other "for richer and for poorer" as they went from rags to riches, and back to rags. When they recovered financially, they went back to riches again.

Rocky and Adrienne always looked deeply into each other's eyes with love, tenderness, and compassion. My favorite line in all the *Rocky* movies was when Rocky described his relationship with Adrienne to her brother by saying, "She's got gaps. I've got gaps. Together, we can fill the gaps."

Rocky and Adrienne never expected each other to read each other's minds. They had honest, open conversations. They defended each other's honor, and they never put each other down. Their most passionate arguments allowed them to experience a meeting of the hearts.

We also witnessed Rocky humble himself by asking a priest for a blessing of protection and strength before he engaged in his boxing matches. Every time Rocky won a championship, it boosted the morale of many people in a very poor neighborhood of Philadelphia who had been rooting for the underdog.

We witnessed Rocky and Adrienne experience the high notes and low notes of their life together until Adrienne departed from this life.

Everything I described regarding Rocky and Adrienne's relationship to each other (and to the Lord) made them winners at the game of life and love in the hearts and minds of millions of viewers throughout the world.

There were so many good messages from the movie, *Rocky*, that I wanted my children to absorb. Unfortunately, the movie also conveyed the message that it is alright to take big risks with one's brain for love of a sport. At the time, I assumed that all my children were smart enough to pay no mind to that message and realize that these types of things are only supposed to happen in the movies!

One of the things I genuinely appreciated about sports was how they helped my highly exuberant children channel their energy in a positive direction. Unfortunately, one of those sports badly injured one of my children. My intentions were good. However, I can't help but wonder, where did I go wrong as a mother?

I pondered that question for a while and came to realize that I should have made it clear to my children that their brains were a lot more important than their bravado. As I analyzed the choices that I made as a mother and peered more deeply into my soul, I could see that there were times when I admired my children's bravado. For better and for worse, I nurtured their bravado. I nurtured it by allowing them to watch movies like *Joan of Arc* and *Rocky*. I nurtured their bravado, even more, when I allowed them to play in combative sports. I didn't realize how much it could or would backfire on one of my children.

Charley knew that I did not want him to resume wrestling after he was released from the hospital. He went against my fully expressed wishes. I admit there were times when I made a deliberate attempt to raise my children to be courageous and to have a fighting spirit. I wanted my children to fight for what is good, and when necessary fight their own demons, not fight against me! Now, I feel the need to fight back, or I should say, "fight for what is good!"

The way I am fighting for what is good is by writing a book that teaches people how to win the game of life and love, which does not necessarily have anything to do with playing or winning in sports. Then again, maybe it does, at least in part.

I've reached a place in my life where I feel a great need to follow my heart. I hope and pray that which is stirring inside my heart is being stirred by the Lord.

On that note, let's take a music break to listen to the song, "Follow Your Heart" with Anthem Lights.

CHAPTER 23

For the Love of the Athlete

About a year and a half after Charley started having seizures, the movie, *Concussion*, was released to theaters. It's based on a true story about a forensic pathologist named Dr. Bennet Omalu who performed an autopsy on Mike Webster, a well-loved center, known as "Iron Mike," who played for the Pittsburg Steelers and the Kansas City Chiefs.

Iron Mike was only fifty years old when he died. The forensic pathologist determined that the cause of Mike Webster's self-destructive behaviors, which led to his premature death, was due to highly destructive proteins that formed inside his brain and caused him to exhibit symptoms associated with severe mental illness.

Dr. Omalu and a small group of medical doctors were stricken with grief when they observed a pattern in which many football players in the NFL exhibited self-destructive tendencies associated with mental illness, which in turn led to their premature deaths. An autopsy performed on three of the Steelers determined that the highly destructive proteins wreaked havoc on all their brains.

As time went by, more autopsies were performed on professional football players who died at an early age. Their autopsies tested positive for the highly destructive proteins as well.

Dr. Bennet Omalu, the physician who performed the autopsies, concluded that the human brain isn't equipped to withstand repetitive blows to the brain. When the brain is traumatized time and time again, the brain forms highly destructive proteins that strangle the healthy brain tissue in the brain.

After careful review, a select group of medical doctors agreed with Dr. Bennet Omalu's findings. They co-authored and published an article in a prestigious medical journal based on Dr. Omalu's research and named the degenerative brain disease "chronic traumatic encephalopathy."

High-ranking officials of the NFL became alarmed and outraged when they learned about Dr. Omalu's study. They thought Dr. Omalu was giving football a bad reputation. They did not want the public to find out how lethal football could be.

In the movie, *Concussion*, one man screamed, **"If only ten percent of the moms decided that football is too dangerous for their sons, it would be the end of football!"**

I realized after watching the movie three times that the statement about ten percent of the moms did not have to be in the movie. Out of curiosity, I read the book, *Concussion,* written by Jean Marie Laskas. I could not find the line about ten percent of the moms in the book. This told me that the statement was the screenplay writer's way of sending a message to mothers that it is within our power to prevent our sons from playing football, or any high-impact sport especially when they are young.

Since the time the movie, *Concussion,* was released, Dr. Bennet Omalu has also written two books which can help parents make informed decisions regarding their children's involvement in many sports. One book is named, *Truth Doesn't Have a Side: My Alarming Discovery of Contact Sports.* Dr. Omalu has written another book called, *Brain Damage in Contact Sports: What Parents Should Know Before Letting Their Children Play.*

I read both books within three days. They held my interest and were very informative. Every parent owes it to their children and to themselves to read Dr. Omalu's books before making any decisions about their children's involvement in sports. If time constraints are preventing you from reading his books, I urge you to read one article he has written that can be found on the internet. It is called, *Opinion/Don't Let Kids Play Football – The New York Times 2015/2017.* Dr. Omalu did a great job of covering a lot of territory in one article that he wrote shortly before the movie, *Concussion,* was released.

Just like Dr. Omalu, I want to point out to parents that **it is not only concussions that we have to be** concerned about, but also repetitive sub-concussive blows which also damage the brain. The percentage of concussions and sub-concussive blows need to be taken into consideration when evaluating the safety of any sport.

I appreciate the tremendous amount of personal sacrifices Dr. Omalu made to conduct his research and share his knowledge with anyone who desires to learn about brain injuries through the articles and the books that he has written. Dr. Omalu is a first-class angel of wisdom who has made many personal sacrifices to conduct his research and to share his knowledge about the dangers of contact sports.

Halo Hint

Sharing knowledge and standing up for truth are outstanding qualities of a first-class angel.

Being the voice of reason requires a person to possess heroic virtue in that he or she may experience severe criticism and persecution for their willingness to share knowledge and tell people things which they may not want to hear.

I have immense respect for Dr. Omalu and the information that he has shared. However, I also realize that his words of wisdom can easily create a conflict of interest for many parents and coaches. Instead of talking to parents and coaches about their conflict of interests, I would like to discuss my mine.

I want to start out by saying that I enjoy socializing with people during football games. Southerners seem to love football even more than Northerners. Now that I am a Southerner, inviting people over to watch a football game now and then is an easy way to nurture my friendships. When we invite friends over for football games, it gives me the opportunity to showcase my cooking skills and be "the hostess with the mostess." This poses a conflict of interest because I know, thanks to the movie, *Concussion,* that football players can easily end up with severe brain damage.

I am also married to an Auburn football fan, which causes another conflict of interest. For the sake of our relationship, I feel it is important to take an interest in my husband's interest. I cannot avoid taking an interest in Joe's interest because when Joe is at home, he lives and sleeps in Auburn t-shirts.

Joe and I love to reminisce about the Iron Bowl of 2013 when Auburn won against Alabama in the last second of a tie-breaker after Alabama fought to have one second added to the clock while they had possession of the ball. Sports announcers said that it was the most amazing upset in college football history. Joe and I love watching old video clips of that game. However, I also want to point out that the game wasn't won in the last moments with brawn. It was won with the brains of the coach, Gus Mazlan, who told Chris Davis to stand in the end zone just in case the field goal was missed, and the speed of Chris Davis who ran like a madman from one end zone to the other. If you have never seen this amazing play, you have to see it for yourself. Just do a web search for the ending of the 2013 Iron Bowl.

Ever since the Iron Bowl of 2013, Joe and I have made a hobby of collecting Auburn paraphernalia. I have an Auburn necklace and an Auburn ribbon for my hair for game days. Joe and I also have an Auburn room in our house with orange curtains and Auburn Tiffany lamps. We even named our dog Aubie after the Auburn mascot.

Every time I watch the movie, *Concussion*, I become even more aware that my desire to bond with my husband, family, and friends by watching college football with them has a way of overshadowing my concern for the wellbeing of the Auburn college football players as well as the players on the opposing team. How can I continue to allow football to be a part of my love life and social life, knowing that so many football players' brains are maimed every time they go out on the football field?

Now that I have exposed my duplicity, I also feel the need to confess one of my quirkier characteristics. I have a difficult time giving any football game my full, undivided attention unless it is an exciting game like the Iron Bowl of 2013 that grabs my attention and sustains my attention. In all honesty, I have never watched an entire football game from start to finish without my attention being diverted to other things. The last Auburn football game that I attended, I asked Joe if we could leave the stadium during the third quarter. Auburn was winning by a wide margin. I felt as though I was going to die of boredom.

When I watch an Auburn football game on TV with Joe, I enjoy watching parts of the first and the last quarter. During the second and third quarters, I enjoy reading or writing, catching up on some laundry, preparing a meal, washing the dishes, or talking to anybody who is willing to talk to me.

I admire male strength, speed, and endurance as much as any other woman. But, my admiration of a man is based on who he is as an entire person. I become bored when I am required to focus only on a man's physical attributes for a long time. It is a man's mind and heart that keeps me interested and captivated.

If I could change the game of football, it would have only two quarters instead of four quarters. This would cut the game in half, which in turn would give everybody more time to have heart-to-heart conversations and do other important things. Here's the kicker. If every football game was cut in half, it would cut the amount of time that a football player could get injured in half!

Another option to accommodate football enthusiasts might be to have four separate strings and allow each athlete to play for only one quarter. Just imagine the momentum of a football game if coaches put the fourth string in for the first quarter, the third string in for the second quarter, the second string in for the third quarter, and they saved the best football players for the last quarter! It would make the game much more exciting!

One day I pitched my idea to cut football games in half to a small group of men. They had a good laugh. I laughed with them. However, I still like my idea. That's why I pitched it again in this chapter.

I'm just getting warmed up. I have another idea that I'd like to pitch for the game of baseball. As you may have guessed, I do not have a long attention span when I watch baseball games either. However, I think nine innings is the perfect number because there are nine baseball players on the team. It would be interesting to see what would happen if nine players on a baseball team were required to play all nine positions by changing positions each inning. It would teach children how to make smooth transitions, how to be flexible and versatile, and how to adapt to changing conditions. It would also teach children how to place themselves in somebody else's position. These are very important life skills which every child needs to learn.

Another interesting way to play baseball with older, more seasoned baseball players would be to require the pitcher, the catcher, and the shortstop to rotate positions every inning. The infielders would be required to rotate positions every inning, and the outfielders would be required to rotate positions every inning. Everybody on the team would play three different positions, three times per game.

We know that pitchers are more inclined to get shoulder and elbow injuries. Catchers get the most concussions and experience more strain on their back and extremities than any other player. By rotating positions, the pitcher, catcher, and shortstop would place less wear and tear on various parts of their bodies. The chances that the pitcher/catcher/shortstop would get a concussion would be reduced by about 66.6 percent if he/she only had to be a catcher for a third of the game. It would also give the pitcher/catcher/shortstop multiple opportunities to analyze batting styles from more than one vantage point. They would also utilize different parts of their brains. Switching positions would provide in-fielders and outfielders with a change of scenery. It would make the game more interesting for them to play.

I hope there soon will come a time when men, women, and coaches will agree that it is in the best interest of children to restructure the way sports are played to reduce injuries and make every sport safer for athletes of all ages. I hope schools and universities will follow suit.

On that note, let's take a music break to listen to the song, "Hold Us Together" by Matt Maher.

CHAPTER 24

Wow, Just Wow!

Right when I thought I had made my final edits for this book, I read Dr. Bennet Omalu's books. When he said children under the age of eighteen should not play high-impact contact sports, my eyes almost popped out of their sockets. The main reason I had a difficult time adopting Dr. Omalu's philosophy was that I had a hard time imagining what my sons' childhood would have been like if I had prevented them from playing football and wrestling.

A Walk Down Memory Lane

I would have loved to have been a baseball and tennis family. However, my children's desire to play baseball and tennis didn't last long. They seemed to possess an internal compass that guided them to sports that offered more excitement. Soccer was more exciting for them than baseball and tennis.

After my children played soccer for a few seasons, Tommy started making urgent requests to play football. I told him that I could not sign him up for football, while his siblings played soccer because I was only one person and their father worked a lot of hours. After I explained the situation, Tommy continued to make his desire known.

In the meantime, a little girl on Charley's soccer team developed a crush on him. She was the soccer coach's daughter. Charley started getting preferential treatment from the coach. One day the coach offered to pick up Charley at our house for practice. I was always running late, and he wanted to make sure that Charley was on time. I accepted his offer and did not notice that the coach was the most handsome man in town until he showed up at my doorstep to pick up Charley. The following fall, I signed Tommy and Charley up for football instead of soccer. Protecting myself from coveting another woman's husband had always been on my radar. Unfortunately, something as important as protecting my sons' brains was not on my radar.

Halo Hint

Protecting the things which are the most precious to us should always be on our radar whether it is our soul, our marriage, or our children's brains.

Tommy and Charley played football enthusiastically from the moment they set foot on the field. Their faces beamed with love for the game even after they were placed on the second string.

My first marriage ended at the beginning of the football season the following year. I signed Johnny and Tony up for football that year with the hope that football would serve as a "healthy distraction." It did not work. My little guys had a hard time understanding why they rarely got to play football.

The following year, Johnny told me that he wanted me to sign him up for soccer instead of football. I told Johnny that I had to keep all my sons in the same sport because I was only one person, not two. I promised Johnny that he could play soccer, but it would have to be in the spring.

When Tommy and Charley were in seventh and eighth grade, I got the impression that they were recruited to wrestle by their fitness instructors. Wrestling swiftly turned me into a celebrity mom. Every time I went to a meet, people told me how much they loved watching Tommy and Charley wrestle. Their wrestling team provided them with a sense of belonging to a family that was not broken. Tommy and Charley felt loved, respected, and admired by their peers and many members of our community. After my younger sons watched their older brothers wrestle for a few seasons, they wanted to wrestle too.

When we moved to Destrehan, Louisiana, I told Johnny and Tony they would have to get involved in indoor sports and activities because I couldn't handle the humidity and hot temperatures. There is a reason LSU's football stadium is called Death Valley!

Joe played racquetball with my sons at a health club while I swam in the pool. After I acclimated to the climate, I relaxed my rules and allowed my sons to get involved in outdoor sports. Tony and Johnny played baseball. By the time my children and I adapted to Destrehan, Louisiana, it was time for us to move to northwestern Louisiana.

Tony decided to give football another try when he was in eighth grade. He enjoyed the intense exercise that he got during practice but rarely played during the game. None of my sons ever got to play much football. They opted out of football on their own. My oldest son, Tommy, played football longer than his brothers because he got more playing time.

My younger sons wrestled in high school even after their older brother ended up in the hospital for seizures. At the time, I adopted the philosophy of a doctor that said, "Sports are good until they aren't good for you anymore." I also rationalized that wrestling in Louisiana was like wrestling for a second or third-division school. However, even one of my wrestlers in Louisiana got a concussion. I told Tony that he was done wrestling for the season to give his brain a chance to heal.

After I thought about Dr. Bennet Omalu's books for a few weeks, I realized that it would have been better if I had exposed my sons to a variety of sports and allowed them to be a master of none, except for the safer ones. Unfortunately, I exposed my sons to many sports, and I provided them with ample opportunities to master two of the most dangerous sports--football and wrestling.

At this time, I would like to share a list of other sports and activities my children participated in during their youth:

Blowing raspberries, blowing bubbles, ballet, bicycling, swimming, hiking, sledding, ice-skating, roller-skating, rock climbing, tree-climbing, weightlifting, calisthenics, jumping on the trampoline, **jumping fences, jumping in puddles, throwing tantrums, throwing themselves onto the floor, thrashing, kicking, tickling, torturing, climbing out of bedroom windows, pulling doors off the hinges, running away from home, roof climbing, new construction inspection,** building sandcastles, building forts, carousel riding, pony riding, horseback riding, camel riding, elephant riding, John Deere riding, dirt-biking, four-wheel riding, go-carting, basketball, bowling, miniature golf, disk-golf, Frisbee, hula-hoop, hopscotch, jump rope, rope climbing, badminton, volleyball, fishing, flying kites, down-hill skiing, water skiing, surfing, water polo, shooting pool, croquet, bocce ball, air-hockey, darts, ping-pong, paintball, snow shoveling, snowball fighting, making angels in the sand and the snow.

After reading the list of activities my first-class angels in training were engaged in, can anybody understand why I was willing to try anything and everything to keep them out of trouble?

Since reading Dr. Omalu's books, I have undoubtedly gained an appreciation for his words of wisdom. I can't help but wonder if there was a memo that went out when my children were younger that told parents that we needed to sign our children up for sports that not only kept them out of trouble but their brains out of trouble too. Maybe there was a memo that went out, but my head was stuck up in the clouds when the messenger delivered it.

Two More First-Class Angels

Just before I published this book, I woke up one morning and suddenly remembered that my brother Lou said a long time ago that he wasn't going to allow his sons to play football due to the high incidence of concussions. I recalled that I briefly overheard his conversation in passing back in the early 1990s. I was not a part of the discussion Lou had with his friends because I was too busy reveling in the joy of being a new mother. I do not recall which baby I was holding in my arms, but it was probably my daughter.

Lou's children had to have been very young when he was creating a game plan for his sons. He decided that instead of playing football, his sons would play soccer. His sons were also engaged in other activities such as scouts, swimming, water polo, hiking, downhill skiing, and playing the piano.

Today, my nephews are happy, successful adults who are winning the game of life and love. Each one has a beautiful wife or beautiful woman that wants to accompany them on life's journey. My nephews also have prestigious jobs that require them to use the analytical part of their brains. Lou and Sue are first-class angels and winners at the game of life and love in that they did an excellent job of raising four wonderful sons.

I spoke to Lou more recently about his decision to require his sons to play soccer instead of football.

Lou said that he still regards soccer as being a contact sport because soccer players still get concussions. Dr. Omalu has analyzed the game of soccer, and he offers parents and coaches strategies to make soccer a safer sport. Turning his strategies into reality would require a grass-roots effort on the part of fathers and mothers.

Halo Hint

Working at the grass-roots level to make a sport safer is a noble undertaking of a first-class angel.

Are Soccer Players High Achievers?

I signed Maria up for soccer with her younger brothers when she was about seven years old. She was a good little soccer girl and played through high school. I would have been tickled pink if Maria had become a school teacher, but she decided at a young age that she wanted to become a doctor. I believe playing soccer increased Maria's determination, self-discipline, and self-confidence—three qualities that were needed for her to become a doctor.

According to an article in Men's Health, there might be a connection between playing soccer and high performance outside the soccer field. To get a better idea, you can read an article written by Cassie Shortsleeve called, "Why Soccer Players Are Smarter" at menshealth.com. It says professional soccer players are in the top 2 to 5 percent of the population regarding executive function and creativity, according to a study done by Predrag Petrovic, Ph.D., the lead researcher, and professor of Karolinska Institute, located in Sweden. The article was written on April 12, 2012. It's a little outdated. However, if more researchers determine that soccer increases intelligence, all schools should make soccer a higher priority.

Parents and schools should evaluate each sport based on its ability to increase a student's intelligence. Funding should go toward the sports that are most likely to increase a student's intelligence. If it is true that soccer increases intelligence, it would not be difficult for a grammar school, high school, or a college to transform a football field into a soccer field.

Go Vintage!

I want to encourage young parents to rediscover the fun of vintage games and other activities with their children. I was amazed a few years ago as I watched how much fun a group of neighborhood kids had while playing croquet in my yard. My two younger sons, Johnny and Tony, found an old croquet set that nobody was using stored in my garage. Several children showed up to play croquet every day for about two weeks. Every so often I stepped outside and watched the kids having fun as they immersed themselves in the game of croquet. Badminton, volleyball, ping-pong, and miniature golf are great family-bonding games that are affordable. If you want to be a little more progressive, you can also play disk-golf or Frisbee with your children!

Theater Is a High Impact Sport

I encouraged the arts and nurtured them with my two younger sons and would have enjoyed seeing all my children be a part of more school plays. It takes a lot of courage to say one's lines on a stage, sing, dance, or play a musical instrument in an auditorium in front of a large audience. Public speaking and stage fright are the greatest fears in life that many adults work hard to overcome. Why not encourage children to do it while they are young?

My son Johnny was embarrassed that he was the only one out of his four brothers that was interested in theater. I said, "Don't worry about it. Remember what Shakespeare said, 'The world is a stage, and we are the actors.'" Those weren't Shakespeare's exact words, but my son got the picture. So many people are influenced by what they see on TV and the movies that acting should be regarded as a high-impact sport. Actors, actresses, newscasters, priests, ministers, teachers, song artists, and those who possess the courage to speak in public or vlog are perfectly positioned to impact the masses.

A Mother's Prerogative

After Charley's medical crisis, I told Johnny and Tony that if they experienced one concussion, they were no longer allowed to wrestle. Compared to my other children, Tony has been the least involvement in sports. For that reason, I seriously considered retracting my words. During Tony's year of recovery, I remained undecided about whether or not I would allow him to wrestle again. I finally made up my mind that I wanted my youngest son to find something else to do with his time other than wrestling. Although it is late in the game for my family, I will explain my new and improved position on sports in the next chapter.

On that note, let's take a music break to listen to "A Mother's Song" by T Carter Music.

CHAPTER 25

Heads Up

If anybody needs a heads up about the dangers of high-impact contact sports, it is the mothers of young children. I want to discuss this topic with fathers too, but I have a feeling that mothers will be more receptive. I am armed with the knowledge that mothers are the ones who usually sign the consent forms for their children to participate in sports. Mothers do much of the driving to and from their children's activities. Therefore, mothers carry a lot of authority as it pertains to children's involvement in sports.

I am also aware that a mother might inadvertently relinquish her authority when she feels pressured to allow her child to play a sport due to her spouse's love of a sport, or a child's desire to play a sport. It is for that reason that I would like to provide young mothers with a sample game plan for their children that I hope will lower their risk for injuries.

I feel the need to assure mothers that you do not have to worry that you are going to emasculate your sons by following this game plan. Utilizing muscles in any sport will enable testosterone levels to remain high. If you want to ensure your son's masculinity, you can also invest in a pull-up bar and tell your son to do daily pull-ups.

The game plan I propose will take some effort, but it will be fun especially if you do your best to work with your child instead of relying solely on the coaches.

Before you get started, you should read through the entire game plan to get acquainted with it. Every so often you should review the game plan to stay on track.

SAMPLE GAME PLAN

- Ladies should pray for your child's father to go along with the game plan before you execute it, and while you are executing the game plan.

- If you do not know much about tennis, baseball, basketball or soccer, you should get to know them by studying the rules while your child is a baby or a toddler. Take the time to watch games on TV to gain an appreciation for these sports.

- Pray often that your child will be safe while playing any sport.

- When your child is in preschool or sooner, sign your child up for swimming lessons and tennis lessons.

- Swim with your child and play in the pool with your child.

- Take tennis lessons at the same time as your child and play tennis with your child.

- Take a lot of pictures of your child swimming and playing tennis. Frame the pictures and put them in places that have a lot of visibility in your home. Also, fill up a photo album with pictures of your child swimming and playing tennis. Make a big fuss over their ability to swim and play tennis. Do your best to make swimming and tennis your "favorite family sports."

- While your child is mastering swimming and tennis, read Dr. Omalu's book, *Brain Damage in Contact Sports: What Parents Should Know Before Letting Their Children Play.* Spend some time studying it so you can discuss it with other mothers. It is a short book and an easy read.

- Recommend Dr. Omalu's book and my book to other moms to build camaraderie with them.

- After your child has learned to love swimming and tennis, you can introduce him or her to baseball and basketball.

- Pray for your child's safety before each sports event.

- Do not sign your child up for flag football. It might awaken in your child a desire to play tackle football.

- Have fun developing or improving your athletic skills with your child/children.

- If your child's father states that he wants to sign your child up for football or another combative sport, watch the movie, *Concussion*, with your child's father.

- After the movie, introduce your child's father to Dr. Bennet Omalu's book, *Brain Damage in Contact Sports: What Parents Should Know Before Letting Their Children Play*. Discuss the book with him.

- If you are not in a relationship with your child's father, give him a copy of the movie, *Concussion*, and Dr. Omalu's book, *Brain Damage in Contact Sports: What Parents Should Know Before Letting Their Children Play*, for Father's Day. When an opportunity presents itself, discuss the movie and the book with him.

- Tell your child's father that you want your son or daughter to play in competitive sports, but you do not want him or her to participate in combative sports. After seeing the movie, *Concussion*, and reading Dr. Omalu's book, chances are good that your child's father will not want your child to play football or combative sports.

- If your children's father isn't on board, tell him that you possess strong convictions concerning brain health. Stay calm and hold your ground.

- Tell your child's father that you would rather see your child play soccer than tackle football and that you would rather see your child play baseball and basketball instead of combative sports.

- The best time to introduce your child to soccer is after he or she has mastered swimming and tennis, and he or she has learned how to play baseball and basketball.

- Sign your child up for soccer **during the fall season, so soccer interferes with the football season**.

- The likelihood that a child will experience a concussion increases when a child plays two seasons of the year. Offset the risk of concussion and sub concussive blows by allowing your child to play soccer for only one season instead of two or more seasons.

- Allow your child to play no more than one organized sport per season.

- Insist that your child learns how to play at least one musical instrument, so he or she realizes that there is more to life than playing sports.

- Consider allowing your child to take one season off per year from sports, or tell your child that you want him or her to participate in sports every other season to give him or her more time to focus on school and other hobbies.

- Tell your child that you want them to be a well-rounded individual and explain what that means to you.

An advantage to playing more than one sport is that it will minimize the likelihood that your child will develop an addiction to one of those sports. Granted, he or she might not obtain a sports scholarship but will have gained the skills to play intermural sports in college, which in turn will alleviate your child's stress levels.

I have never been a fan of traveling teams because I regard them as being time thieves. I didn't realize what a mistake it was when I made a concession for Charley and allowed him to join the wrestling traveling team. Wrestling in school and being on a traveling team enabled him to be involved in a sport year-round where he was taking repeated blows to the head. A no-off-season approach to wrestling also caused my son to develop an addiction to wrestling.

Even if a child does not play a combative sport, it is not a good idea to allow him or her to become overly attached to a sport because there is a good chance that he or she will become depressed when it is time to retire from their favorite sport. The last thing a person needs as they make their transition into adulthood is to experience post-sports depression. There is always a big let-down when an athlete's playing days are over.

However, if your child/children developed a love for swimming and tennis when they were young children, they will always have swimming and tennis to fall back on when it is time to retire from another one of their favorite sports.

If you take enough pictures, your child's earliest memories will be of him or her swimming and playing tennis. The warm feelings which your child associates with swimming and tennis will help them feel less depressed and less deprived when it is time for them to retire from another sport.

Show & Tell

- If your child wants to play a combative sport, **watch the movie, *Concussion*, with him or her.**

- After the movie, **discuss the movie with your child** and **explain to your child that concussions cause brain damage, repetitive blows to the head can cause brain damage, and any blow to the head can damage the nerves in the brain which are extremely delicate.**

- Have your child listen to the kids' brain song that you listened to in an earlier chapter.

- Explain that some sports can cause more serious blows and more repetitive blows to the brain than others.

- After your discussion, **show your child the book**, *Brain Damage in Contact Sports: What Parents Should Know Before Letting Their Children Play."* Point out the author's name on the cover of the book.

- **Tell your child**, "I've read this book from cover-to-cover, and the sport you want to play is one of the sports that Dr. Omalu says is harmful to a child's brain. For that reason, I cannot allow you to play this sport."

Dr. Omalu is most concerned about children and wants our society to gain a greater love and respect for children's brains. My son happens to be one child whose brain was seriously injured by participating in a combative sport. Dr. Omalu's book written especially for parents teaches us that every child's brain can be seriously injured while playing high-impact contact sports. It does not matter if symptoms begin to manifest when somebody's child is seventeen, twenty-seven, thirty-seven, or older. When symptoms occur, the child is still our child!

Dr. Omalu calls football, hockey, wrestling, and some others, "high-impact contact sports." I prefer to call them "combative sports" because it is a more accurate term. The nature of combative sports is to make physical contact with one's opponent, to bring them down, or physically move them out of the way to score points.

Athletes who play combative sports can easily become desensitized to pain. They are trained to overlook their body's warning signs and will keep playing after they have been injured. Back-to-back injuries or a series of injuries that occur in a short period can cause significant damage to the athlete's brain or their spine.

I refer to baseball, basketball, tennis, soccer, track, volleyball, swimming, bowling, and golf as "competitive sports." Athletes involved in competitive sports avoid physical contact with their opponents. Physical contact with another player might occur in competitive sports, but it is never intentional.

Halo Hints/Winning Tips

Competitive sports encourage athletes "to play smarter" instead of "playing rougher." Playing smarter is what every person needs to win the game of life and love at any stage of the game.

I've told my son's story. In the telling of his story, I have come to realize that this story is not only about what happened to one of my sons. This story is about every son or daughter who participates in a combative sport. If a parent's decision to protect their child's brain and their life adversely affects the game of football, hockey, wrestling, or any combative sport at the college or professional level, it is not a parent's problem. It hits home too hard when a sport severely injures our child.

I'm not angry at any combative sport. I'm angry at myself for not creating and executing a better game plan for my sons when they were young. However, I know everything happens for a reason. God can take an unfortunate event and turn it around for the good of many people. (Genesis 50:20)

I hope and pray all parents will arrive at a place where they will feel extremely uncomfortable watching their child participate in a sport where their brain is being battered repetitively. If you are feeling uncomfortable, do not ignore what your heart, mind, and spirit are telling you.

Let's pray that God gives all parents the wisdom and courage to say what must be said and do what must be done to protect their children's brains and all their God-given potential.

Dear Lord, I hope and pray that You will give parents the wisdom and grace to execute an amazing game plan to help their children enjoy sports and other activities that will be the perfect blend of safety, fun, adventure, and camaraderie.

Please allow sports and other childhood activities to assist children in the development of their emotional, physical, mental, and spiritual growth. In Jesus' name, we pray. Amen.

On that note, let's take a music break to listen to the song, "Have It All" sung by Jason Mraz.

CHAPTER 26

Bless Your Heart

Some reasons parents from all over the world want their sons and daughters to participate in sports is because we know those sports help our children dodge other bullets. There are a lot of battles to be fought during childhood. There's the battle against thugs, drugs, and alcohol. There's the battle against the excessive use of video-games and social media. There's the battle against pornography and promiscuity. There's the battle against boredom and the bulge. Sports enables parents, children, and their coaches to fight those battles together! Moreover, everybody needs mental toughness to survive the assaults of daily living.

No matter what experiences life has brought us or taught us, we want our children to be strong and courageous. However, another important question to ask ourselves as parents is, what kind of strength and courage do we want our children to possess? As I stated in a previous chapter, I want my children to possess the same kind of strength and courage that Saint Joan of Arc possessed.

It is important to point out that Joan of Arc was a pious and prayerful young woman who never participated in aggressive sports activities and was not trained for combat before she entered battle. Her strength and courage to fight for her faith, her family, and her country came from the Lord.

Joan's love of the Lord combined with her love of France and her desire for her country's men and women to have the freedom to freely express their Roman Catholic faith was so immense that she changed the course of history by loosening France from the stronghold of England near the end of the Hundred Years' War.

At first, the Roman Catholic Church and many people of France were grateful to God for Joan's courage to speak to the young King Charles and persuade him to step into his rightful authority as king of France. The French became even more enchanted with her bravery when she joined the soldiers and went out on the battlefield against England. During that era, it was believed that women had no place on battlefields. Joan's bravery greatly increased the morale of the French soldiers and enabled them to win more than one battle.

Unfortunately, in less than a year's time, King Charles and the hierarchy of the Roman Catholic Church became disenchanted with Joan when she began to offer them strategies to win back all of France from England. King Charles and the Catholic Church began to doubt the sincerity of Joan's motives. In a short period, she went from being perceived as a heroine to being viewed as a reckless zealot who was breaking command. Moreover, church officials began to doubt the origin of Joan's visions of saints and angels who told her that she had been called by God to free not just part, but all of France.

After questioning her in a trial, Roman Catholic Church officials from France and England arrived at the verdict that Joan was operating under the demonic influence and had to be burned to the stake as a heretic and a witch. The error of their ways was revealed to them when Joan's heart remained bleeding on the stake after the rest of her body had burned to a char! Her incorrupt heart was believed to have been a miraculous sign from God that Joan of Arc's heart was full of love, her intention to do the right thing was pure, as was her desire to do what God commanded her to do.

The miracle of Joan's incorrupt heart strengthened France's resolve that God was on their side. The French soldiers and militia fought with greater intensity and succeeded in winning back all of France from England.

Joan of Arc taught us that love of God, family, and one's country can motivate an individual to fight for justice, endure severe persecution, and brutal death to stand up for what one believes. However, much of history has also taught us that hatred, pride, as well as an unjust desire for power, can also motivate a person or a group of people to fight with brutality and misdirected courage to destroy their opponent.

Each of us can choose to be motivated by selfish gain, hatred, vengeance, and an immense desire to control and overpower other people. We can also choose to be motivated by love, justice, and a desire to provide freedom and good living conditions to citizens of our country and to people from other countries who are reaching out to us for help. Each of us can choose to be interiorly motivated by that which is good or by our vices. However, scripture tells us that love conquers all! (1 Corinthians 13) Therefore, if we want our children to grow up to be strong, courageous, and willing to fight for all that is good, it is our duty as parents to assist our children in doing the kinds of things that will increase their capacity to love.

On that note, let's take a music break to listen to a song called, "Good Fight" by Unspoken.

CHAPTER 27

Fall into the Pool of Love

For nine years, my family lived around the corner from my brother, Lou, and my sister-in-law, Sue. When Charley was three years old, Lou and Sue built a beautiful in-ground pool in their backyard. I can still picture Charley fearlessly jumping off the diving board at a young age. My children and I had great times hanging out at Lou and Sue's pool. To this day, my children and I love visiting their Uncle Lou and Aunt Sue because we can feel their love.

However, my children and I feel an even greater loving connection with Lou and Sue in the summer months when we hang out at their pool. Even after we moved away, Lou and Sue graciously extended their hospitality by allowing me to use their backyard to host graduation pool parties for my children throughout the years. That makes Lou and Sue first-class angels and winners at life and love in my book.

Halo Hint

A willingness to open's one heart and pool to family and friends is a fantastic quality of a first-class angel.

While growing up, I received a lot of hospitality from friends and relatives when they opened their hearts and their pools to me. My parents extended a lot of hospitality to family and friends when my brothers and I invited cousins and friends to swim in our pool too. As a young person, I envisioned that I would have a pool in my backyard when I grew up. I wanted to have fun in the sun with my family and friends in my very own pool.

Before we got married, my children's father and I spent some of our time hanging out at a pool at his apartment. While we were courting, we talked about having a pool of our own one day. After we got married, we talked a bit more about having a pool. However, we never got a pool of our own because our backyard was shallow. We also thought a small above-ground pool in our yard would not compete with the large in-ground pool that was in my brother's backyard, which was just around the corner.

Jumping Back into the Pool of Love

Four years after my former husband and I split up, I met Joe. We dated, we courted, and we got engaged. Then Joe's job took him away. We broke off our engagement to think things over. A few months later Joe invited me to Louisiana to figure out if it was possible for my two younger sons and me to acclimate to life in Louisiana. At the time Joe was living in an apartment complex that had a pool. Joe and I went for a swim in the pool. We splashed around in the pool. We talked while we were in the pool. We had warm, fuzzy feelings while we were in the pool.

I said, "This is nice. I would love to have a pool."

Joe said, "Nobody is using this pool right now except the two of us. If we get married, we can move to a subdivision that has a pool and enjoy a pool that we won't have to maintain."

Two years into our marriage, Joe and I moved to a subdivision that was making plans to build a pool. A year later, our HOA let us know that it would not build a pool in our subdivision until it finished building houses on all the empty lots. When I found out about the delay, I said, "Oh Joe, could we get a pool? We've waited long enough."

Joe said, "I don't think so. A pool is a lot of work."

To keep the peace, I did not push the issue.

A couple of years later, Joe's brother Michael and our sister-in-law Emily decided to have a beautiful in-ground pool built in their yard. Joe and I started spending more time at Michael and Emily's house. Michael, Joe, Emily and I were happy that our pool time together was fostering a more loving bond between our families. However, our drive to Michael and Emily's house in Texas is three and a half hours. It wasn't too long before I started gently nudging Joe to get a pool, often resorting to the use of puppy dog eyes.

One day I said, "I have been waiting my entire adult life for a pool, and I want at least two of my children to experience what it would be like to have a pool in our backyard. Swimming is my favorite exercise. It helps me to feel more alive."

Joe relented and said, "After I sell my Corvette, we'll get a pool."

Joe kept his promise, and I am honored that he was willing to make such a big sacrifice for the love of our family. Joe also does most of the upkeep on the pool. Pools need chemicals, and Joe's background is in chemical engineering. For that reason, pool mainte-nance fell into Joe's department. Joe's loving sacrifice and his willingness to use his gifts and talents for the good of our family is what makes Joe a first-class angel and a winner at the game of life and love in my book!

Halo Hint

Making sacrifices and using one's gifts and talents for the love of one's family members is an amazing quality of a first-class angel.

Bonus Halo Hint

Taking on added responsibilities and carrying them out with love in one's heart is a beautiful attribute of a first-class angel.

Our oval above-ground pool is big enough for us to swim short laps across the pool or bigger laps around the pool. Creating a whirlpool is fun. Then we turn around, and swim in the opposite direction, against the current. On hot summer days, I enjoy taking writing breaks by jumping into our pool with my children and the neighbors. Joe and I also enjoy our nightly swims after dinner. After a good workout, we float around in the pool and talk. Our pool dates foster better communication between us. I'd rather spend time with Joe in our pool than eat out at a fancy restaurant. Our pool dates help us to feel a lot more connected, and they also help us to stay in sync with each other.

When my son Johnny comes home from work or his other activities, he likes to jump in the pool to blow off steam and hang out with me. We swim around the pool. Then we wade in the pool and talk about what's going on in his life. My son Tony sometimes manages to pry himself away from his video games, every so often, to hang out with his friends and me in our pool too!

Bonding in the pool with my children and my husband allows us to have a more loving connection. Our pool also helps us to form closer relationships with our neighbors and friends. I have one friend who told me that hanging out at my pool was a lifesaver when she was going through a difficult time in her life. Our pool is helping our family to build a sense of community in our little neck of the woods, at least until the HOA builds a pool in our neighborhood.

Halo Hint/Winning Tip

Every family needs to have a pool or easy access to a pool because pools have a way of "pooling" people together. Pools provide a sense of unity and community. Having a pool or having easy access to a pool is like having a little piece of heaven on Earth!

Decorating Tips

You don't have to hire the Pool Kings to have a nice pool in your backyard. There are a lot of photos on Pinterest that show us how to make a relatively inexpensive pool look very inviting! I saw one small round pool that had a Hawaiian grass skirt wrapped around it. You can find hundreds of pool ideas online to create a loving, tranquil atmosphere in your backyard. I purchased some nautical decorations at Hobby Lobby and Cracker Barrel for our pool. Joe and I enjoy swimming and relaxing in our private paradise.

Halo Hint/Winning Tip

The ability to turn one's backyard into a paradise is an awesome skill of a first-class angel which isn't too difficult to develop, especially if you hit the sales.

Here are eleven reasons why families should make swimming a favorite family pastime, and why our schools and communities should work to make swimming a favorite national pastime:

- Swimming can be an indoor or an outdoor sports activity. When the weather is pleasant and warm, athletes can swim outside. When it is cold out, athletes can swim inside.

- Swimming is one of the safest sports. There is no need to wear a helmet when swimming. If a person joins a swim team, they will only need to wear a swim cap.

- One can swim with their head in the water or above the water and still get a good workout by utilizing most or all their muscles.

- Swimming forms lean, elongated muscles.

- Swimming is a great form of exercise that can help people get in shape by strengthening the core muscles.

- Swimming builds endurance and can be used as a form of cross-training.

- Swimming at a fast pace is a great cardiovascular workout.

- Swimming is a great form of exercise for people of all ages.

- Swimming is easy on the joints.

- Hanging out in a pool fosters good communication in that people do not carry their cell phones, their computers, or their video games into the pool! Good communication enhances relationships by allowing people to have heart-to-heart conversations to create a stronger, more loving bond.

- Swimming at a slow pace or just wading in the pool is a great stress reliever. We live in a stressful world. Parents and children need something natural that relieves their stress, tension, and anxiety. Too many people in our country are too worked up and on edge about many things. An overall feeling of wellbeing would increase in our country if more people spent time chilling out in swimming pools.

Bonus Halo Hint

Falling into the pool of love would solve many world problems.

On that note, let's take a little music break to listen to Bobby McFerrin sing the perfect pool song, "Don't Worry Be Happy."

CHAPTER 28

Tennis Anyone?

As a young mother, I enrolled my children in tennis lessons and took some tennis lessons myself. However, my desire to play tennis with my children got derailed as soon as I signed my children up for soccer. If I could press a replay button and be a young mother all over again, I would have made sure that my five children had become good little tennis players before I introduced them to other competitive sports.

It wasn't until I started writing this book that I realized that tennis is a sport that was designed to foster loving relationships. I should have had this epiphany a lot sooner because when people play tennis, the score starts out "love-love!"

There is a lot to love about tennis, once we get to know the sport a little better! I am providing twenty great reasons why more families should endeavor to make tennis a favorite family pastime, and why our schools and communities should work to make tennis a favorite national pastime.

Tennis can be an indoor or an outdoor sports activity. When the weather is pleasant, it is good to get some sunshine and breathe fresh air by playing tennis outdoors. When it is miserably hot or cold outside, there is the option to play indoor tennis.

No helmets are required when playing tennis.

Tennis provides numerous health benefits and increases endurance.

Tennis can be used as a form of cross-training.

Tennis teaches young children how to have sophisticated coordination which is excellent for brain development.

Learning how to play tennis increases an athlete's ability to excel in other sports in that tennis requires an athlete to have good hand-eye coordination, good ball judgment, speed, agility, and endurance.

Tennis is good for parents who have children with ADHD in that it keeps an overly active child "caged in" so parents can chase after the ball instead of their wild chicken!

Married couples can play doubles with their children.

If you are a single parent, you can play singles with your child or each of your children.

Tennis allows you to convey the message that you are "cute and adorable" or "athletic, and confident."

Tennis allows you to be completely in control of the signals that you send your opponent. You could also psych out your opponent by sending mixed messages.

Tennis is a sport that many people can play well into old age.

Tennis fosters a strong sense of friendship and camaraderie.

Tennis allows children and parents to take turns watching each other compete with their peers. That way children will not grow up thinking the world revolves around them.

Tennis places parents in a position to tell their children that they want equal playing time or at least some playing time!

We need to keep in mind that adulthood is typically a lot more stressful than childhood. Therefore, adults need to get an adequate amount of exercise and play time to alleviate their stress levels.

In our society, parents love honoring their children by supporting them in their sports activities and cheering for them. However, children are just as capable of honoring their parents by supporting them in a sports activity by cheering for mom and dad. Tennis could be used to teach children the importance of reciprocation (otherwise known as give and take) in their most important relationships.

On that note let's take a little music break to listen to the song "One Love" sung by Blue.

CHAPTER 28

Exercising the Heart Muscle

Doing something good for other people brings us great joy and a tremendous amount of personal satisfaction. According to an article written by Bill and Rich Sones in the Wisconsin State Journal, dated Saturday November 17, 2007, "More than 50 studies at 44 major universities and funded by Case Western University Medical School have shown that generous behavior will reduce your risk of illness and mortality, and that benevolent acts have a deep and lasting impact on mental health, with these protections still intact decades later." The title of the article was "Giving to others means a happier, healthier you."

I remember what was going on in my life many years ago when I read that article. I was a newly divorced, single mother of five children. I was no longer in a position where I could afford to take my children on costly vacations to Disney World or hit the slopes with them in Colorado. However, I knew that doing little things with my children often brought greater joy than living large.

One of the little things that we did was spend one day and one night at the Wilderness Resort in Wisconsin celebrating a string of November birthdays in my family. I can still remember the tremendous sense of wellbeing I felt that weekend even though the only birthday gift I was able to give to two of my sons and my nephew was the gift of a one-day/one-night stay at a resort that welcomes children.

There was a photographer in the lobby that was taking photos for a small fee. I gathered the three boys and had a picture taken of them feeding a real baby tiger a bottle filled with baby tiger formula. Until this day, it is one of my favorite photos.

Another little thing that brought joy to my heart was that I cut out the article about the rewards of giving that Bill and Rich Sones wrote in the Wisconsin State Journal. I placed the article inside of my purse for safekeeping, knowing that someday I might want to refer to it in my book. I had just started dreaming about becoming a published author. Then I forgot all about the article that I tucked inside my purse.

About six months before publishing this book, I found the yellowed newspaper article inside the purse I hadn't used in years while cleaning out my closet. The newspaper article survived four moves in eleven years! When I read the article a second time, it brought a smile to my face just like it had done the first time I read it many years ago when I took a one-day trip to the Wilderness Resort with my two oldest sons and my nephew.

Someday when I am gone, one of my sons is going to snatch up that picture taken in the lobby of the Wilderness Resort and keep it for themselves. They are going to find the little article about the ***importance of giving*** tucked inside of a little plastic bag taped to the back of the picture.

The authors of that article wrote, "Giving is the most potent force on the Earth" and provided a short list of simple things we can do to be a part of that force. "Paying a compliment, telling a funny joke, sending a thank-you note, listening to someone attentively, donating to a hunger center, teaching a child to read, (and) extending forgiveness to someone who has wronged you."

The article affirmed what I already knew deep inside my heart. We do not have to do extraordinary things to make ourselves and other people happy. We can provide ourselves and other people with a lot of joy just by doing a lot of little things with great love!

I was able to experience a measure of joy and contentment even after I experienced the heartbreak of a divorce because the one thing that remained a constant in my life was that I was still living under the influence of Saint Therese of Lisieux. She was a nun who died in her early twenties but was regarded by more than one pope as one of the greatest saints of modern times. In her memoir which she wrote for her sisters, Saint Therese said that she thought she was incapable of doing great things due to her fragility and inadequacies. However, it did not prevent her from believing that

Jesus loved her a great deal because of her willingness to do ordinary things with great love and make a lot of little sacrifices. She offered her little sacrifices and everything that she did to Jesus for the conversion of people who did not know, love, or serve the Lord. Her main mission in life was to console the heart of Jesus as she tried to do a lot of little things to make Jesus and other people happy.

Saint Therese's style of spirituality is known as "The Little Way." I embraced The Little Way a long time ago because I realized that I was just an ordinary person who possessed a lot of shortcomings and weaknesses. I experienced peace and consolation as a young person when I learned from Saint Therese that I could make God happy and other people happy while being an ordinary person who strives to follow The Little Way.

I felt the need to explain The Little Way because many of the halo hints that I have provided are not anything more than little loving gestures that anybody can do. A person who aspires to do great things might regard many of the halo hints as insignificant. However, we must never forget that a lot of little things that we do on a daily basis have the potential to have a big impact on the people around us in that all of the lakes and the oceans are made up of a lot of little droplets of water, many splinters of wood form a mighty tree, and many tiny cells come together to form plants, animals, and human beings.

Halo Hint/Winning Tip

Doing all things with love is a primary function of a first-class angel.

On that note, let's take a music break to listen to a song called, "Dream Small" by Josh Wilson.

CHAPTER 30

Amen!

Dr. Daniel Amen is an elderly doctor who looks like an angel and knows what it is like to fight for brain health. He is a psychiatrist who has written a book called, "The Brain Warrior Way" which he wrote with his wife, Tanya. In the book, Dr. Amen said when he was in his thirties that he envied the brain scan of his mother who was in her sixties. He believes the reasons his brain was in poorer condition than his mother's brain was that he played football in high school, contracted meningitis when he was in the military, and he had some other bad habits that harmed his brain.

I assume some of those bad habits had to do with what he ate because there is also a cookbook that accompanies "The Brain Warrior Way" that Dr. Amen coauthored with his wife, Tanya.

As a comfort food queen, I have reached a time in my life when I feel the need to eat humble pie in that it has become all too obvious to me that nutrition plays an important role in maintaining not only a healthy heart but also a healthy brain. Having been a former owner of a fitness center, I've known about the importance of good nutrition for a long time. There was a time in my life when I got the results that I wanted just by avoiding processed foods and performing relatively easy exercises.

Desperate times called for desperate measures. After my divorce, I said goodbye to health and fitness and decided that I wanted to be "the ultimate comfort food queen" to bring comfort to my children. Bringing added comfort to my children was one of those things that I never thought would backfire on one of my kids. Charley suffers in that the chances of him having a seizure increases when he indulges in certain types of foods that used to bring him comfort.

Charley has been told by more than one doctor and nutritionist that he should be on a ketogenic diet. I feel bad for my son, knowing that it takes a lot of self-discipline to remain on a diet that is not comprised of comfort foods even though some foods on a ketogenic diet are very tasty and satisfying.

As for Moi

To this day, I love rich food and heartier portions. For those two reasons I do not know that I will ever evolve into a health food guru. However, I have also come to realize that I cannot be a comfort food queen every day of the week. I can't even have an all-weekend love affair with food without feeling as though I have poisoned my body by the time Sunday evening rolls around.

God knows how much I miss the days when I could eat to my heart's content and go into a food coma for an hour or two when I was in my teens and twenties.

In my early thirties, I was able to eat to my hearts' content on the weekends, watch what I ate during the week and lost the weight that I gained over the weekend.

In my mid-thirties, things slowly began to change. I had no choice but to add some exercise to my routine if I wanted to remain comfortable in jeans.

I took a fall in my mid-fifties while walking my dog and my knees started giving me trouble. My fifties have been filled with happiness because I married a man that loves me through thick and thin. However, there comes a time in everybody's life when our bad habits finally catch up with us. In my late fifties, I have come to realize that I must make my health a higher priority if I want to continue living a high-quality life.

I love listening to Dr. Amen on his YouTube videos. I also love when he reprimands us, using a gentle tone of voice; saying things like, "There are certain things that we love to eat, and there are certain things that we love to do that don't love us back."

Dr. Amen uses a brain scan called SPECT imaging. When reading the scans, he and his team of specialists can tell a patient which parts of their brain are functioning properly, and which are functioning poorly. He and his team of specialists have assisted many patients that have brain damage caused by addictions to foods, alcohol, drugs, and even sports.

The doctors at Amen Clinics offer strategies to assist patients who are experiencing such things as lack of focus, memory loss, poor brain function, post-traumatic syndrome, or chronic traumatic encephalopathy to improve their brain function.

Dr. Daniel Amen is also more than happy to share much of his knowledge and love for the brain on his YouTube videos and the books that he has written. That way, even a person who never becomes a patient at Amen Clinics can take steps toward improving their brain health.

Dr. Daniel Amen, Tanya Amen, and their staff possess a strong desire to help people of all ages who are struggling with poor brain function. They offer education, hope, and help to those who want and need it. That makes all of them first-class angels and winners at the game of life and love.

Halo Hint

Educating people about brain health and helping people improve brain function are extraordinary undertakings of a first-class angel.

Many of us struggle with different kinds of addictions and obsessions. We can only do what we are supposed to do or stop doing what we aren't supposed to do by educating ourselves and seeking out first-class angels who want to assist us. We also need the help of God's grace to change bad habits into good habits.

On that note, let's take a little music break to sing or listen to a song called, "Chain Breaker" with Zach Williams.

CHAPTER 31

When the Dream Ends

After my son was released from Holy Name Hospital, he was extremely distressed that many of his memories had vanished and his ability to learn and retain information had decreased. The thought that he might not be able to wrestle again only made matters worse. That summer, Charley told his brother Tommy that he was going to kill himself. No sooner those words left his mouth, Charley took off like a bat out of hell and started running toward a busy intersection. Tommy went chasing after Charley.

For just an instant Charley looked back over his shoulder and noticed that Tommy was lagging behind. For some reason, it tickled Charley's funny bone that his older brother seemed to be in worse physical condition than himself. Instead of throwing himself in front of a moving vehicle, Charley sat down on the ground and had himself a good laugh. I am so grateful to God that Tommy was there for Charley and saved his life by using a comic relief maneuver!

Halo Hint

Saving a life is a heroic undertaking of a first-class angel.

About a year later Tommy went on active duty with the military and protected an American naval base overseas. My family and I thank God that he came back safely. We continue to pray for Tommy's safety as he plans to go on active duty again. Tommy's immense desire to protect his family and his country makes him a first-class angel and a winner at the game of life and love.

Halo Hint

A desire to protect people and our nation are outstanding qualities of a first-class angel.

Charley had legitimate reasons for being depressed after he began having seizures. First, he spent several weeks detained at three different hospitals. Then he spent an entire year at home recovering while his friends went away to college. When I stand back and look at all the anguish that my son experienced, it makes more sense as to why he felt such a strong desire to fall back on a sport that he loved. Some athletes love a sport so much that they would rather die than stop participating in their favorite sport. Unfortunately, Charley was one of them. I've learned from my son that nobody can make an athlete retire. It is something that must come from within their own heart.

There is also scientific evidence that suggests that athletes can become addicted to adrenaline, endorphins, and dopamine that their bodies produce when they engage in sports activities. If an athlete ends his or her career abruptly, he or she might experience withdrawals which can show up in the form of depression. Even when an athlete retires from a sport of his or her volition, there is still a possibility that he or she will experience depression. The athlete's family members must pray that the Lord will help an athlete find a new purpose and a new reason for getting up out of bed every morning.

A Fun Coping Mechanism

If it is time for you to retire from a sport that you love, you will need to replace it with another pleasurable activity. When the body stops moving one way, it is important to get the body moving another way to prevent depression.

Singing and dancing is something that has always helped me to overcome depression. I found an interesting article posted from a 2008 American Science magazine called, "Why do we like to dance—and move to the beat?" written by Columbia University neurologist, John Krakauer. To make a long story short, listening to music and dancing stimulates many regions of our brain and allows us to experience two forms of pleasure at the same time. The neurologist referred to the experience of listening and dancing to music as "a pleasure double play." His article tells us that if we do anything to music, we can experience "a pleasure double play." We might be able to experience a pleasure triple play by doing two things at the same time while listening to music.

It is difficult to remain depressed when it within our power to produce a natural form of blissfulness. With that thought in mind, I'd like to provide a short list of things we can do to experience a pleasure double play, or a triple-pleasure play to help us overcome depression due to the end of any dream:

- Driving down a scenic highway while listening to the radio allows us to experience a pleasure double play.

- Sunbathing while listening to music allows us to experience a pleasure double play.

- Cooking while listening to music allows us to experience a pleasure double play.

- Writing or journalizing while listening to music in the background allows us to experience a pleasure double play.

- Cooking while listening and singing to music allows us to experience a triple-pleasure play.

- Listening to music, while singing and dancing allow us to experience a triple-pleasure play.

- Swimming in the pool while listening to the music and basking in the sun allows us to experience a triple-pleasure play.

The last bullet point is particularly useful in producing a natural high because it provides us with exercise therapy, music therapy, and sunshine therapy all at the same time! If you do some of the activities mentioned above with another person, those activities will be even more enjoyable.

Any time we experience a major disappointment or one of our dreams comes to an end; it is important for us to do things that help us to enjoy life once again. The easiest way to enjoy life is by indulging in life's simple pleasures.

An athlete can also replace his or her favorite sports activity with another recreational activity. Bo Jackson serves as a great example. When he could no longer play professional football or baseball, he took up archery and began exercising other parts of his brain and body. There's something extremely rewarding about developing a new skill that revitalizes our spirit. Taking on a new hobby such as painting or learning to play a musical instrument can revitalize a person's spirit. Recreational sports such as swimming, tennis, golf, beach volley ball, kayaking, and other water sports are fun activities that can provide a tremendous feeling of wellbeing.

When a person is trying to rewrite the story of their life, they must spend time engaging in pleasurable activities to help them get their creative juices flowing. Doing things to get the "creative juices flowing" will help a person figure out what they want to do with the next phase of their life when their playing days are over.

Anytime a dream of ours comes to an end; it is good to take on a new hobby or develop a new skill. When I went through a divorce, I decided that I would one day become a published author.

I spent many years writing before I was able to figure out a way to get my books published. However, my new dream gave me renewed vitality. My dream to one day be a published author helped me to feel as though I was embarking on a new adventure. My new dream also helped me to stop viewing myself as being a loser in life and love, and it helped me to strive to be a winner in the game of life and love.

The sports maxim, "Every athlete dies twice" came to my attention while I was writing this chapter. Some people believe that an athlete experiences death when he or she retires from a sport, and once again when he or she passes from this life to the next.

I refuse to accept the maxim because an athlete is not meant to die when he or she retires from a sport any more than a person is meant to die after they go through a divorce. Retiring from a sport is like going through a divorce in that an athlete must end a relationship with the love of their life. However, after each heartbreak or setback, God wants us to have a great comeback!

Athletes are not meant to die after they retire from a sport. Virtues like: courage, strength, determination, self-discipline, and perseverance which an athlete developed while playing a sport do not die when an athlete retires. Nobody can take those virtues away from an athlete, even if he or she is seriously injured. An athlete can utilize his or her virtues for as long as the athlete lives to give him or her the winning edge in many aspects of life!

One reason an athlete should look forward to the next season of their life is that all the time and energy that they invest in a sport holds them back from discovering their many other gifts and talents. Also, a sport that takes up a lot of time can easily compete with a person's most important relationships. After a person retires from a sport, it should be easier for them to have a life that is more balanced and more rewarding than they ever imagined.

There comes a time when an athlete must change the same way that a caterpillar changes into a butterfly. The athlete does not die when he or she retires, as long as he or she changes and learns how to fly to a higher realm of love!

On that note, let's take a music break to listen to the song, "I Believe I Can Fly" with R. Kelly."

P.S. I Believe I Can Fly" was one of Charley's favorite songs when he was a little boy! I believe all athletes are meant to fly to a higher realm of love when they retire from their favorite sport.

CHAPTER 32

A Great Lover & Fighter

My generation and the generation that preceded mine got to see how life played out for the world-renowned boxing champion, Muhammad Ali, who lived from 1942 to 2016. Many of us old-timers enjoyed watching him dance around the ring and dominate his opponents. Our spirits soared with his during his glory days. Our hearts went out to him in a different way, filled with sadness when we had to watch him struggle with Parkinson's disease after he retired from boxing.

I was young when Muhammad Ali was a champion boxer, and I was in awe of his strength and confidence. However, I did not get to see the sweetness that resided inside his spirit until I read some articles about him after he died.

In one article, his daughter Hana Ali said, "Helping strangers in need had always been his insatiable drive." The article went onto say that Ali tried to use his fame to uplift and inspire people all over the world.

Hana Ali's fond memories of her father pulled on my heartstrings and made me want to learn more about the life of Muhammad Ali. First, I googled his name and read about his life in Wikipedia. I also watched some short video clips of his life on my computer.

A while later, I found a book on Amazon that Muhammad Ali wrote called: *THE SOUL OF A BUTTERFLY: REFLECTIONS ON LIFE'S JOURNEY.* The name of the book brought a smile to my face as I recalled that I had already referred to a butterfly in my book when I wrote, "There comes a time when an athlete must change the same way that a caterpillar is changed into a butterfly. The athlete does not die when he or she retires, as long as he or she changes and learns how to fly to a higher realm of love!"

Muhammad Ali, king of the boxing ring, was known for saying, "I float like a butterfly and sting like a bee!" I remember hearing his chant on national TV when I was a child. Based on the title of his book which he wrote, he must have related more to floating like a butterfly than stinging like a bee after he retired from the boxing ring. If any athlete's life story can teach other athletes how to retire and fly to a higher realm of love, it would be the life story of Muhammad Ali! His life story can also teach athletes how to retire with dignity and class.

Muhammad Ali's memoir arrived at my front door one spring day at about three o'clock in the afternoon. I cracked open the book and couldn't put it down until I read it from cover to cover. As I was reading, I also realized that Ali's main purpose in life was bettering other people's lives. He set up a legacy where he could continue bettering people's lives, long after he died by building the Muhammad Ali Center, an interactive museum in Louisville, Kentucky. Muhammad Ali's dying wish was to help people from every walk of life achieve greatness.

Muhammad Ali was raised in a Christian home by a Southern Baptist mother and a father who was a Methodist. Both of his parents showered him with love, attention, and affection which enabled him to have a lot of love, confidence, and self-respect. During the times in his childhood when he and his family were subjected to racism, it did not change the way he felt about himself or the way he viewed his skin color. He thought black was beautiful. Prejudice did not drag him down, because the love he received at home helped him to recognize his value.

His parents' love which they conveyed to him helped him to recognize the value of all human beings. His mother and his father taught him that hating is wrong no matter who does the hating.

Although his family attended services regularly at a Baptist church, Christianity was off-putting to him in that pictures of Jesus had always been depicted to him as being a white man. Ali also noticed that all of Jesus' apostles were white men and the skin-color of the angels were white as well. His observations as a child caused him to wonder if black people were allowed in heaven.

Ali also noticed as a child that there were not any black superheroes. It was for that very reason that he made up his mind at a young age that he would become a role model for black children when he got older. He succeeded in becoming a superhero and role model when he won a gold medal for boxing in the 1960 Olympics.

Halo Hint

Striving to be a good role model for children is an outstanding quality of a first-class angel.

Muhammad Ali received a hero's welcome when he returned home from the Olympics. He was proud of his great achievement. One of the reasons he set his sights on winning the gold medal was not only to be a great role model for black children but to win equality for his people.

Halo Hint

Seeking justice and equality for people is an extraordinary undertaking of a first-class angel.

Shortly after winning the gold medal, Muhammad Ali and his friend went to a restaurant in his hometown.

When the waitress came to their table, she let them know that they were not welcome to dine there. Ali politely introduced himself to her as the Olympian champion. She stepped away to speak with her manager. When she returned, she told Ali and his friend that they couldn't stay at the restaurant! Ali felt the sting of rejection when he realized that winning the gold medal did not change the way whites perceived him and his people. Out of pain and frustration, he threw his gold medal into a river!

I got the impression from reading his memoir that Muhammad Ali was drawn to the Islamic religion because he looked up to African-American Muslim religious leaders. Moreover, Malcolm X and Elijah Muhammad were happy to serve as his mentors and spiritual directors. It should not be surprising that Ali embraced a religion which he associated with black people who loved and embraced him, and he rejected the Christian religion which he associated with white people who had previously enslaved his ancestors and rejected him on a personal level even when he demonstrated that he was worthy of love, respect, and admiration. Moreover, Muhammad Ali made it clear in his memoir that he was extremely hurt when he and his friend were told to leave the restaurant. It was one of the reasons he did not want to remain a Christian.

While reading about Muhammad Ali's life, I also learned that his birth name was Cassius Marcellus Clay Jr. He changed his name to Muhammad Ali during his early twenties to free himself of a name which he believed had been handed down to his family by a slave owner. Ali's name change took place shortly after he became a Muslim. Muhammad Ali was the name he was advised to take by Elijah Muhammad. Elijah Muhammad was an American born citizen who led the Nation of Islam (an African American political and religious movement) from 1934 until he died in 1975.

Although Muhammad Ali's conversion to the Islamic religion seemed divisive in the eyes of many, he exercised his right as an American citizen to choose his religion and believed that the Muslim religion was a peaceful one.

He stood up for peace and love, like many young people during the 1960s and 1970s. He used his freedom of religion once again to avoid fighting in the Vietnam War. His conviction to be a peace-loving man came at a high price when his title as boxing champion of the world was revoked.

Even though he was a great fighter, Muhammad Ali's desire for peace was genuine. The wars that took place among people of different countries, races, and religions did not make sense to him at any juncture of his life. He believed that if we believe in God that we should also believe that God wants us to live in peace and harmony with each other. He worked hard to be a messenger of love and peace throughout his adult life, and he regarded it as his greatest accomplishment.

He strove to portray himself as a formidable fighter to intimidate other boxers, but he was an undercover first-class angel who possessed a gentle spirit which he intentionally kept hidden from his opponents. Unbeknownst to other boxers and to the world, Muhammad Ali custom-designed strategies for boxing on the offense and on the defense that were intended to wear out his opponents and cause as little physical harm to them as possible and, at the same time, protect his pretty face!

Ali believed that he had done such a good job of avoiding being hit in the head that boxing was not the main cause of Parkinson's disease. He claimed that many people who never box end up with Parkinson's disease.

Although I would like to believe that Ali was able to dodge many blows to the head, I do not know that it is true. My Uncle Tony, who followed Muhammad Ali closely, said Ali was very good at avoiding being punched when he was a young fighter, but toward the end of his career, Ali took more punches to the head.

When Muhammad Ali was diagnosed with Parkinson's disease, he became depressed and was frustrated by the way disease slowed him down. However, his strong prayer life, his faith in God's goodness, and his belief in God's plan for his life gave him the strength that he needed to carry on.

It also saddened Ali that Parkinson's disease changed the way he spoke, but he said that it turned him into a better listener. Ali did his best to maintain a positive outlook on life and wanted to be a good example to people who suffer from all illnesses.

Muhammad Ali had some healthy habits. He tweeted on August 28, 2012, "No pork, soda pop, cigarettes, alcohol – ever!" His healthy habits conjoined with his strong desire to help people enabled him to be a loving, compassionate person during his entire life. Ali served others through numerous acts of charity, and by being a messenger of peace and love on a local, national, and international level.

What I admired the most about Muhammad Ali while reading his memoir was that he always possessed a clear vision of his life's mission from the time he was a child. As the seasons of his life changed, he would set new goals for himself, and take on new missions. However, his main mission in life always encompassed wanting to make a difference in the lives of other people.

Halo Hint

Loving people and making a difference in the lives of people are important aspects of a first-class angel's job description.

Ali believed that we should discuss our religious beliefs to gain a better understanding of each other and find common ground. Most importantly he believed that we need to live in peace and harmony as we love each other even when we do not hold the same beliefs or opinions. All these things and so much more made Muhammad Ali a first-class angel and a winner at the game of life and love!

Wouldn't it be just like God to inspire a man known for having been such a great fighter throughout the world, to be a messenger of love, peace, and prayer in a world that is in such great need of it? Just like Saint Francis of Assisi and many saints throughout the ages, Muhammad Ali was given to us as a gift from God to teach us how to win the game of life and love!

Some Christians believe that Jesus gives nonbelievers a chance to accept Him as their savior shortly before or after they die. I believe this to be true, especially when a non-Christian goes out of his or her way to demonstrate their love to God and other people. Jesus made it clear that God is genuinely pleased with anybody who plays the role of The Good Samaritan as indicated in Luke 10:25-37. Jesus also made it clear that those who take care of the poor, the down-trodden, and the broken-hearted will be judged mercifully. (Matthew 25:35-40) There are many interpretations of the Bible, but I get the impression that people who are devoted to serving others with love in their hearts pull heavily on God's heartstrings.

Muhammad Ali lived Christ's messages of love better than many people who call themselves Christians. He picked up his cross and carried it after he got Parkinson's disease. While he was carrying his heavy cross, he reached out to people in need and gave them a helping hand. His daughter, Hana, testified that "Helping strangers in need had always been his insatiable drive." That's why I believe that as Muhammad Ali released his last breath, Jesus took him by the hand and revealed Himself to be His Savior and the Only One who can set him free from the slavery of sin and death!

On that note, let's take a break to listen to **Wintley Phipps explain the history behind the song, "Amazing Grace" at Carnegie Hall**. Wintley Phipps did a great job of teaching an important lesson in American history, which I hope will be made known one way or another to all Americans. He also did a great job of singing the song.

If like me, you believe that love conquers all, and in the end, good will prevail, then it makes sense to do something good every day of our lives, even if it is only one small act of kindness. It makes sense to act like an angel of mercy when we meet a person in need of assistance or encouragement. It makes sense to interact peacefully with every person we meet. It makes sense to offer an olive branch when we disagree or we have stepped on somebody's feet. It makes sense to be the most loving person that we can be.

As we strive to be first-class angels, let's remember that God is love and mercy, and we have been made in God's likeness and image. Until we see God face-to-face, let's keep in mind something Muhammad Ali once said to his daughter Hana, **"It is only the heart that makes us great or small."** There are many great quotes from Muhammad Ali, but that one is the greatest of them all!

On that note, let's take another music break to listen to the song, "Put a Little Love in Your Heart" sung by Jackie DeShannon.

CHAPTER 33

Glory to Glory

When I was a young person, my friend Angela talked me into trying out for cheerleading. I had a hard time learning the cheers, but with help from my friend, I became a part of "the cheerleading squad," as we called it back then.

The first year that I cheered and every year after that, I was selected to climb to the top of the mounts. Every year the mounts kept getting higher. The summer between my junior and senior year in high school, we broke a record at a competition by building the highest mount in Illinois. The year after I graduated from high school, regulations restricting the height of mounts were put into place for the safety of the cheerleaders. For that reason, nobody ever broke my squad's record.

If I had fallen off one of the mounts, I could have broken my back or cracked my skull wide open. I was able to overcome my fear of danger because I loved basking in the glory once I got to the top of the mounts.

I am not sure why I was selected to climb to the top of the mounts. There were other cheerleaders on my cheerleading squad who were just as tiny as me and just as light on their feet. The only thing that makes any sense to me (pardon my vanity) is that I could have won an Olympic gold medal for having the cutest legs on the planet.

When I was a cheerleader in high school, I was aware that I risked my life every time I climbed a mount. God was merciful and spared my life even though I was puffed up with pride and vanity. I believe the main reason God spared my life was that my life was not meant to end as a cheerleader.

Nobody's life is meant to end during or after the height of their sports career. God has a game plan for every season of our lives. However, it is our job to know ahead of time when a season is nearing its end. That way we can begin preparing for the next season.

I decided to quit cheerleading when the football season ended during my senior year of high school when I could have cheered through the basketball season. I called it quits one season early because I woke up one day and realized that cheering was not getting me anywhere.

I took harder classes during my junior and senior year than what I had taken during my first two years of high school to prepare for college. I took the harder classes because I thought they were going to help me to get somewhere.

I wasn't picky about colleges, but I had no desire to attend a community college. To my dismay, taking harder classes lowered my grade point average. My ACT score was humiliating. My humbling experience helped me realize that I was a better candidate for secretarial school.

My transition into the workplace was not easy. I encountered many angry eyebrows the first few years due to my oversights. After I learned the ropes, I became bored being a secretary. I changed fields every couple of years, to mix things up a little, and make my life more interesting. Being a secretary helped me in many ways.

- It enabled me to purchase my first car.

- It taught me how to dress for success.

- It provided health insurance.

- It paid for my vacations, and it provided "paid vacations."

- It enabled me to dine at fine restaurants and become a food critic.

- It exposed me to interesting people in the fields of finance, health, law, real estate, and the chemical industry.

- It helped me build a nest egg and make investments.

- It paid for the many weddings that I stood up to and allowed me to be a generous gift-giver.

- It allowed me to get front row, center seats at Chicago Theater and see Aretha Franklin, which gave me respect.

- It enabled me to live in a high-rise apartment in Chicago, and pretend that I was "The New That Girl" and daughter of Marlo Thomas.

- It enabled me to attend Northwestern University and DePaul University.

- It helped me to learn my way around downtown Chicago, and develop "street smarts," which according to my dad, was better than "book smarts."

- It improved my writing and communication skills.

Every so often we have to ask ourselves, "Is this activity getting me anywhere? Is this activity causing me to spin my wheels? Is this activity helping me to fulfill my dreams, my life's purpose, or is it holding me back?"

I feel a need to reiterate that the reason I retired early from cheerleading many years ago was that I realized that it wasn't getting me anywhere. My ability to see the writing on the wall does not mean that I didn't enjoy being a cheerleader. I enjoyed encouraging fans to demonstrate their team spirit. I enjoyed the camaraderie I felt being a part of the cheerleading squad. I enjoyed having an open-invite to parties just because I was a cheerleader. I enjoyed wearing a cute uniform and showing off my cute legs. I loved the attention I got every time I climbed a mount and stole the show.

I fully embraced being a cheerleader for a season of my life. However, I also realized a little sooner than most cheerleaders that being a cheerleader wasn't going to get me anywhere.

I have my father to thank for giving me the insight to know when it was time to call it quits. My father's ability to know when his playing days were over and his willingness to share his story with his children taught me how to recognize when my cheerleading days were over. My father had a way of telling stories about his life that inspired his children and taught us valuable lessons about life and love.

Halo Hint

Teaching valuable lessons about life and love through story-telling is an amazing gift of a first-class angel.

Another Great Lover & Fighter

My father was a champion basketball player who placed Saint Rita High School in Chicago on the map back in the 1950s. He was a legend in his glory days, but also an unlikely candidate to be a basketball star. He was a short, scrawny Italian guy.

My father got a scholarship to play basketball at Saint Ambrose University in Iowa. Obtaining a scholarship was something that rarely occurred in his neighborhood. It was a great honor.

When my father shared his story about why he gave up playing basketball, it went something like this:

"I enjoyed my glory days when I played basketball, but one day I woke up and realized that basketball wasn't getting me anywhere. I had never been the academic type, and I felt ashamed getting passing grades only because my teachers were giving me preferential treatment.

"After playing basketball in college for one year, my conscience told me that I could not continue playing basketball when my time could have been spent making money to help my mother who was working as a seamstress in a sweatshop.

"So, I dropped out of college and joined the army. While I was in Korea, I sent a portion of the money that I made home to my mother and saved as much money as I could to help my mother buy a house when I got out of the army. It had always been my mother's dream to own a house. I wanted to help make her dream come true.

"My sister, Ginger, my mother, and I combined our savings. Together, the three of us purchased a two-flat apartment building in Chicago. It secured a home as well as a source of ongoing income for my mother."

Their heroic undertaking makes my father and his younger sister, Ginger, first-class angels, and winners at the game of life and love in my book!

Halo Hint

Generosity and a willingness to make sacrifices to help make another person's dream come true are outstanding qualities of a first-class angel.

Imagine how amazing it must have been for my grandmother to know that she had not just one, but two children who made sacrifices out of love and concern for her wellbeing. My dad and Aunt Ginger were in their early and mid-twenties when they helped free their mother from the bondage of poverty. Johnny and Ginger were the youngest of my grandmother's six children.

Halo Hint

Helping someone to escape the bondage of poverty is an extraordinary undertaking of a first-class angel.

My dad ended his story by saying, "I gave up basketball because I realized that **winning at life** was much more important than winning a basketball game and reveling in my glory every time I heard the crowd cheer for me."

Bonus Halo Hint

Winning at life and love is more important than winning at anything.

My father also knew that his mother needed financial support. My dad's willingness to step out of the spotlight and give up a sport that he loved took him to a much higher level of glory and love.

While pointing to 2 Corinthians 3:18, Joel Osteen tells us that "God desires to take us from glory to glory." The purpose of playing a sport is to have fun and give athletes a taste of glory and victory. However, God wants to see His children soar to a higher realm of glory and love. Before we can rise to the occasion, we must spend some quiet time alone with the Lord, just sitting on the bench. After the Lord reveals His new game plan to us, He wants us to get off the bench, and do what needs to be done to fulfill God's game plan for our life so that we can fly to a higher realm of love!

On that note, let's take a little music break to listen to the song, "You Raise Me Up" sung by Selah.

CHAPTER 34

Building Up Our Spiritual Muscles

If you feel as though you are not giving your all to The Head Coach, I would like to provide you with a prayer that will help you give your all to Him. This prayer will help you accept Jesus as your Lord and Savior. If you've already done that, this prayer will help you to renew your commitment to Him.

Lord, Jesus I come before you just as I am. I am sorry for my sins, and I repent of my sins. Please forgive me. In your name, I forgive all others for what they have done against me. I renounce Satan, the evil spirits and all their works. I give you my entire self, Lord Jesus, now and forever. I accept you as my Lord, my God, and my Savior. Heal me, change me strengthen me, in body, mind, soul, and

spirit. **Cover me with Your most precious blood, and fill me with Your Holy Spirit! I love you Lord, Jesus. I praise you. I shall follow you all the days of my life. Amen.**

Optional Prayer:
Mother Mary, all the angels, and saints, please pray for me so I will love God with all my heart, all my mind, all my soul, and all my strength, just as you do.

The above prayer is an adaption of the Miracle Prayer that was written by Father Peter Mary Rookey. The only part of the prayer that I changed was the Optional Prayer. Prayers have more meaning for me when I use some of my own words. Feel free to do the same.

I obtained permission from his secretary to place his prayer in my book a few months before he passed away. Father Rookey recommended that people say The Miracle Prayer every day until they truly mean what they say.

Father Rookey said when people say the Miracle Prayer until they mean it, Jesus will change their life in a very special way. Father Rookey didn't say how our lives would change, but The Miracle Prayer has what it takes to transform us into winners in the game of life and love by helping us to be more devoted to the Lord who is our source of life and love.

On that note let's take a little music break to sing, listen, and dance to the song "Made to Love" by TobyMac (2006).

CHAPTER 35

"Love It Up"

Not too long ago, I attended a funeral of an old family friend named Mrs. Barbee. It was a small, intimate funeral, because my old neighbor that died did not have any children, and she was an only child. She was also an elderly widow who did not have any extended family members. However, she was always loving and kind to us, her neighbors.

My favorite memories of Mrs. Barbee were the times that she and her husband took my brother, Ray, the Connor kids, and me on camping trips. She made us pancakes for breakfast on a little stove in her camper during our weekend getaways. The pancakes she made fell apart and were not very tasty. However, I remember that she made them with a lot of love in her heart. I can still picture her smiling face as she attempted to flip each pancake.

Halo Hint

Expressing love for your neighbor(s) and allowing them to be a part of your life can produce joy for you and your neighbor.

Mr. and Mrs. Barbee taught us how to fish, build a campfire, make S'mores, and gain a better appreciation for The Great Outdoors. They also welcomed us into their home whenever we knocked on their front door to play with their pets or to shoot pool down in their basement.

One day, after Mr. Barbee was gone, I stopped at Mrs. Barbee's house to visit her. While we were chatting, she told me that she always wanted to have children, but she had been unable to have any. I had always assumed that it might have been the case, and I nodded knowingly.

Then Mrs. Barbee apologized to me for the times she was in a bad mood during my childhood. She told me that she loved all the children in the neighborhood but seeing us playing baseball in the street often served as a sad reminder that she couldn't have children of her own. She tried to smile through her sorrow and told me that her cat and her dog were like children to her. If she hadn't opened her heart to me, I never would have understood the depth of her anguish that she endured.

Mr. and Mrs. Barbee were devoted to their neighbors, their pets, and most of all, to each other. They were two people who operated as first-class angels even as they carried the burden of their sorrow. They will always be regarded as winners at the game of life and love in my book!

Although Mr. Barbee looked old to me because of his barely-there graying hair and his beer belly, he ended up dying of cancer at an early age. As a widow, Mrs. Barbee traveled across the country in her camper with her pets. She enjoyed meeting up with her friends from her camping club until she started exhibiting symptoms of Alzheimer's disease.

My mother and father, along with our neighbors, Mr. and Mrs. Connor, looked after Mrs. Barbee for many years before she died. When Mrs. Barbee could no longer live on her own, they helped her to sell many of her belongings and freshened up her home so that she would get a better offer. They prayed that Mrs. Barbee would be able to sell her house at a good price. Their prayer was answered. The house sold for more than anyone expected. Then they helped Mrs. Barbee move into a retirement home.

Halo Hint

Assisting an elderly neighbor is an important job of a first-class angel.

As Mrs. Barbee's memory loss increased, they moved her once again to a facility that cared for people with Alzheimer's disease. Before Mrs. Barbee mind failed, she entrusted my mother and Mrs. Connor to pay her bills and manage her financial affairs by giving them power of attorney.

My mother and Mrs. Connor took their responsibility seriously and made sure Mrs. Barbee had the best doctors and exceptionally good medical care. They visited Mrs. Barbee regularly, even after she could no longer recognize them. Before Mrs. Barbee died, they prayed that she would find peace in the next life and made sure a priest gave her The Last Rites.

Those are just a few of acts of loving service that my parents and the Connors performed as first-class angels and winners at the game of life and love.

Halo Hint

Loving one's neighbors and taking care of other people's physical and spiritual needs are important aspects of a first-class angel's job description.

At Mrs. Barbee's burial site an elderly Irish priest in his nineties gently pointed at Mrs. Barbee's dead body hidden inside the casket. He reminded us that one day we would all be in the same place.

Then he asked a simple question: "How do you spell *love*?"

Mr. Connor said, "L-O-V-E."

The priest said, "Good. And how do you spell *live*?"

Mrs. Connor said, "L-I-V-E."

Then the good ol' Irish priest asked, "What the difference between *live* and *love*?"

Mr. Connor shrugged his shoulders and said laughingly, "One vowel," as if to say, "Ok Padre, what's the point?"

The priest smiled and said, "You're correct! There's only a difference of one vowel. The word *live* has *i* in it. *But, the word love* has *o* in it. Most people think they have been placed on the earth to 'live it up,' but, we have been placed on this earth to 'love it up,' by loving God and other people. To love God and others, we have to take *i* out of *live* and replace it with an *o.*"

The ol' Irish priest paused to let us think about it for a moment. Then he went on to say, "We were not placed on this Earth to make me, myself and 'I' happy. We were placed on this earth to make God and other people happy by loving them in a lot of different ways."

Then the priest who looked like he had one foot in the grave winked at us and said, "I hope you'll be able to remember what I just told you. Because before you know it, one day you're going to be inside of a casket just like your neighbor. It's going to happen a lot sooner than you think. Life goes by in the blink of an eye. So, take the *i* out of live and replace it with an *o.* Our life is a lot better when we love God and other people!

If we can remember to follow the ol' Irish priest advice and act on it, we will have the best strategy for winning the game of life and love. All of us will have what it takes to be first-class angels!

On that note, let's take a little music break to listen to the song, "What the World Needs Now Is Love" sung and written by Jackie DeShannon.

CHAPTER 36

Final String of Halo Hints

To laugh often, to win the affection of children,

To earn the appreciation of honest critics and endure the betrayal of false friends,

To appreciate beauty, to find the best in others,

To leave the world a bit better, whether by a healthy child, a garden patch or a redeemed social condition,

To know even one life has breathed easier because you have lived. This is to succeed!

Adaption of Poem by Bessy A. Stanley

I hope the stories of first-class angels, the halo hints, the angel melodies, as well as the Miracle Prayer helped you to feel as though you have what it takes to operate as a first-class angel and win at the game of life and love.

Until God brings us together again, I'd like to leave you with one last angel melody called "The Prayer" with Celine Dion and Andre Bocelli. May God bless you and always assist you on your journey!

Endnotes

"We are each of us angels with only one wing, and we can only fly by embracing each other." by Luciano De Crescenzo. www.brainquotes.com retrieved May 29, 2018

Prelude to Angel Melodies

Quote of Saint Mother Teresa of Calcutta has been used with permission from the Mother Teresa Center of the Missionaries of Charity, granted on May 18, 2018, www.motherteresa.org

Advanced Halo Hints

Saint Augustine, "He who sings once prays twice." Catechism of the Catholic Church, Liguori Publications @1994 English translation for the United States. Page

299, Singing Music, 1156; reference Eph 5:19; Saint Augustine, En. in Ps 72, 1:36, 914; cf. Col 3:16

Sunshine Therapy

Rebecca Janes Stokes, *Science Shows How A Trip To the Beach Actually Changes Your Brain*, epicadventurestherapy.com, posted February 20, 2017

Wallace J. Nichols, *Blue Mind: The Surprising Science That Shows How Being Near, In, On, or Under Water Can Make You Happier, Healthier, More Connected, and Better at What You Do*, Back Bay Books, posted July 21, 2015

Lifting Minds & Hearts Through Music & The Arts

"History of Music Therapy," American Music Therapy Association, found at MusicTherapy.org

Wear A Helmet or Not Wear a Helmet? That is the Question

Peter Landesman, *Concussion*, Columbia Pictures, December 25, 2015.

For the Love of an Athlete

Jean Marie Laskas, *Concussion*, Random House Publishing Group, November 24, 2015.

Peter Landesman, *Concussion*, Columbia Pictures, December 25, 2015.

Dr. Bennet Omalu**,** *Truth Doesn't Have a Side: My Alarming Discovery about the Danger of Contact Sports*, Zondervan, 2017

Dr. Bennet Omalu, *Brain Damage in Contact Sports: What Parents Should Know Before Letting their Children Play*, Neo-Forensic Books, 2018

Bless Your Heart

Michael Alexander Miller, Ronald Parker, *Joan of Arc*, CBC Alliance Atlanta Communication, May 15, 1999

History of Joan of Arc, Wikipedia, retrieved in March of 2018.

History of Joan of Arc, biography.com, retrieved March of 2018.

When the Dream Ends

"Life after Sport, Depression in the retired athlete" found at believeperform.com/wellbeing/life-after-depression-in-retired-athletes. Written by Emma Vickers, Ph.D. Sports Psychology student.

Journey Healing Center, *Adrenaline: A Strongly Addictive Drug with Serious Consequences*. https://journeycenters.com. November 9, 2010.

Shahram Heshmat, Ph.D. *Can You Be Addicted to Adrenaline?* Psychology Today, dated August 8, 2015.

Barry Popik, *The Big Apple: "An athlete dies twice." (Sports Proverbs)*. August 29, 2012. New York City – Sports/Games

Roger Kahn, *"Every Athlete Dies Twice" originated in a book called "The Boys of Summer."* New York, NY: Harper & Row, 1972. Pg. XX:

A Great Lover & Fighter

Hana Ali, "My Dad, Muhammad Ali," Special to CNN, http://www.cnn.com/2011/OPINION/06/19/ali.fathers.day/index.html

Muhammad Ali with Hana Ali, *THE SOUL OF A BUTTERFLY: REFLECTIONS ON LIFE'S JOURNEY,* Simon & Schuster, 2004

Hana Ali with Danny Peary, *ALI ON ALI: Why He Said What He Said When He Said It,* Workman Publishing Co., Inc. 2018

Exercises for the Heart Muscles

Bill and Rich Sones, *Giving to others means a happier, healthier you*, Wisconsin State Journal, November 17, 2007 Page C2, quoted with permission.

Final String of Halo Hints

Adaption of *To Succeed* poem - first-prize winner in a contest sponsored by the magazine *Modern Women* in 1905 written by Bessie A. Stanley.

Counting My Blessings

I am grateful to The Father, The Son & The Holy Spirit, who are the authors of life and love. Thank you for creating me in Your likeness and image.

Thank you for your mercy and numerous blessings, and for giving me opportunities to bring life, love, joy, and peace into the world. Thank you for all the amazing people who have operated as first-class angels in my life and the lives of my children.

I am grateful for my mom and dad for making numerous sacrifices for our family, friends, and neighbors. For raising me in a loving and happy home. Thank you, Mom and Dad, for your example of everlasting love, and for your love and support during the most difficult times of my life. I can never thank you enough for all the help you provided my children and me during the high notes and low notes of our lives.

I am grateful for my husband Joe and my five children, who enrich my life, delight my heart and continuously bring love, smiles, and laughter to my life. Thank you for being such a great blessing to me and for turning my life into a great adventure. Thank you for your patience throughout the many years of my writing journey. Thank you for seeing the good in me, for loving me, and for the ways you have picked up the slack or have compensated for my short-comings.

I am grateful for my stepchildren: Angela, Michael, and Gabrielle. I have always wanted and needed more than just one daughter, and I couldn't ask for a better "big brother" for my sons. I started writing about first-class angels long before your dad and I met. I feel honored and privileged that he brought three more first-class angels into my life. I'm grateful for the good times we have shared, and I look forward to making many more memories with you three.

I am grateful for all of Joe's family members. Thank you for making me a part of your family and for teaching Joe the meaning of love and loyalty. I am grateful for the good times and laughter that we have shared in your homes and your pools.

I am grateful for Raymond, my dear baby brother who advises me as though he is an older, wiser brother.

Thank you, Ray, for your love and support especially during the earliest stages of my writing journey. Thank you for believing in me. Thank you for teaching me how to be a more loving and compassionate person by your words and example. Thank you for the times you attempted to teach me about the guys' perspective.

I wish to extend an extra-special thank-you to Ray, and his beautiful wife, Jill. Thank you for always opening your home to my children and me, for helping mom and dad in my absence, and for your generous support and the huge sacrifices you made during the high notes and low notes of my life and my children's lives. Thank you for teaching us how to blend a family so well that we often forget that all of us are not blood-related.

I am grateful for my dear brother, Lou, and his beautiful wife, Sue. Thank you, Lou and Sue, for your example of everlasting love to my children. Thank you for being there for my family and for taking care of mom and dad in my absence. Thank you for offering us your love and support in hundreds of ways. Thank you for always opening your heart, home, and pool to my children and me, and for your unfailing support during the high notes and low notes of my life and my children's lives. Thank you, Sue, for mentoring me during the years of motherhood, for helping me with my first home birth and for saving my life during post-partum when I wanted to end it all.

I am grateful for my dear brother, John, and his beautiful wife, Kathy. Thank you for your love directed at my children and me, for sharing your hearts and for providing us with "Southern Hospitality." A special thanks to both of you for teaching me how to spread my wings and fly to a distant place for the love of another person.

I am grateful to the father of my children, known as "Allen" in this book. Thank you for being open to life, for the ways you have blessed me, and for the many ways you have blessed our children. Thank you for the important lessons that only you could teach our children.

I am grateful for my children's stepmother. Thank you for the part you played in raising my children or perhaps I should say "our children;" for teaching them lessons and skills that I could not, and for many ways you assisted "Charley" during and after his medical crisis.

I am thankful for Linda Mazur, who assisted me in raising my children for a decade. Thank you, Linda, for sharing many Bible stories and for teaching my children and me about the love of Jesus. Thank you for teaching me how to be a prayer warrior, for listening to me pour out my heart so many times, for praying for me, with me, and for my family any time of the day or night. Thank you for mentoring me as a mother and for your failed attempt to turn me into another Martha Stewart. Lastly, thank you for being a sister and a great friend.

I am grateful for my "Catholic girlfriends" which include but are not limited to Juli Barman, Marie

Coco, Laura Demkowski, Sheri Doyle, Kathy Keane Chigaro, Terese LaRocco, Diane Leyva (my Jewish-Catholic-Christian friend) Lee Ann Marie, Sue Piccione, Lois Skowronski, and Rena Esposito Sheehan. Thank you for being my friends, hanging out with me, being like sisters to me, inspiring me, giving me the confidence to be me, and doing what Catholic girls do best: sparkle and shine like a brand new pair of patent leather shoes, and lighting up the room whenever we're together.

I am grateful for my family members and friends disbursed throughout many regions of the United States. Thank you for touching my heart and my children's hearts in a special way. Even though we cannot be together as much as we would like, I am thankful for the memories we have made and the ones we will continue to make. Thank you for your love, concern, and ongoing prayers.

I am grateful for my soul sisters and Sisters in Christ who have prayed for my children and me, have inspired us, taught us, supported us, or encouraged us throughout the many years. Many of them include: Cathy A'Hearn, Dina Alhayek, Christine Alwan, Mary Alwan, Jeanette Akroush, Mary Amore, Cammy Anderson, Debbie Angelo, Marjorie Ainsworth, Judy Arceneaux, Kelly Renee Baker, Laura Barbee, Linda Balistrella, Juli Barman, Carolyn Barrall, Helena Banach, Lisa Beecher, Mary Becker, Karen Beebe, Nancy Bubica, Theresa Billau, Amanda Bird, Gabrielle Boroden, Judi Bratcher, Marina Brennan, Chris Brindle, Dorothy Bonvillain, Carolyn Boroden, Dorothy Boroden, Emily

Boroden, Mary Josephine Boroden, Molly Boroden, Jennifer Burrus, Dorothy Cafran, Marie Camarda, Marilyn Camarda, Teri Capshaw, Cori Carmona, Katie Carmona, Gerry Castellani, Leslie Castillo, Melissa Carnaggio, Kathy Keane Chigaro, Mary Childers, Kitty Cleveland, Patty Cochran, Julie Coco, Philis Coco, Marie Coco, Marina Coco, Patty Cochran, Angela Colarelli, Rose Collins, Leslie Abbott Cooper, Deloras Connor, Sonia Cox, Camilla Craig, Mary Damiani, Tamara Dant, Eileen Dedcovich, Laura Demkoski, Mary DeRoche, Jean Diamond, Peggy Dietz, Sheryl Anne DeGregorio, Maureen Dillenburg, Donna Dolan, Mary Donahue, Sheri Doyle, Katrina Donsbach, Barbara Driskell, Lisa Drong, Sue Earl, Andrea Earp, Kathy Einerson, Mary Therese Egizio, Sharon Emergy-Bugajski, Kathy Esposito, Charmaine Fair, Christina Cucci Fischer, Cheryl Freeland, Pat Gano, Teresa Gindl, Linda Gindl, Fran Gorden, Carma Gruhlke, Cheryl Giambattista, Jillian Gibbons, Kelly Gibson, Dr. Barbara Golder, Lynn Goodhart, Nancy Gratz, Bernadine Crenshaw, Patty Guenella, Pamala Frederick, Cheryl Freeland, Candy Hamilton, Kristina Hall, Renee Hall, Jane Rafferty Harties, Amy Heimbach, Andrea Hensberry, Donna Hensel, Carolyn Hewlett, Anne Marie Hobbs, Juli Hoffman, Suzanne Hogan, Brenda Hodge, Kim Hopkins, Sheila Hudson, Kathy Hughes, Rosalie Insprucker, Becky Jamroz, Jennifer Jankowicz, Tracy Jelinek, Caren Johnson, Kathy Kane, Janet Klepper, Mary Koykar, Laura Malek-Kurecki, Susan Knowles, Diane Leyva, Diana Lahey, Jamilee Lahey, Terese LaRocco, Patricia Lawlar, Sandy Layfield, Antoinette Linker, Brenda Lites, Teresa Lightfoot, Kathleen Littleton,

Cindy Levigne, Molly Loughran, Lee Anne Marie, Marybeth Madigan, Mary Mahar, Delaney Marti, Jean Maslan, Pam Massay, Colleen Mast, Linda Mazur, Erin McCune, Rene McIlheran, Krushenka Miller, Cherie Mondrella, Sheila Montgomery, Peggy Moran, Jennifer Moore, Donna Murphy, Patricia Murphy, Deloras Murray, Cheryl Neylon, Susan Niven, Renee Lynne Norris, Eileen O'Brien, Mary Olson, Laura Oremus, Rebecca O'Quinn, Laura Oster, Kelly Ottenstrauer, Donna Ottenstrauer, Diana O'Neil, Jennifer O'Neil, Katie-Anne O'Neil, Mary O'Neil, Maureen O'Neal, Patricia Rafferty O'Neil, Erin Owen, Tiffany Owens, Morgan Paintner, Cheryl Pantone, Colleen Pappas, Mary Frances Parker, Carmella Piccione, Frances Piccione, Annemarie Piccione, Samantha Piccione, Susan Piccione, Jill Piccione, Kathy Piccione, Rachel Piccione, Erin Piccione, Elena Perez, Colette Posillico, Susan Powell, Elise Pratt, Laura Prizmich, Jillian Quintana, Patty Radcliffe, Sissy Radcliffe, Maria Radcliffe, Shirley Radcliffe, Cherie Radcliffe, Laura Robinson, Sarah Romanski, Susan Rothwell, Angel Santhoshi, Loraine Schaefer, Susan Schmidt, Rena Sheehan, Cathy Schneider, Lois Skowronski, Christine Sloan, Eva Limbaugh Svigos, Karleigh Smith, Rita Smith, Crystal Standiford, Emily Stanford, Gwen Stuart, Brenda Stegall, Ginny Thomas, Rose Thomas, Cindy Trent-Malcomb, Anne Villapando, Sandra Vickers, Jaime Waddell, Sandra Ward, Holly Witte, Regina White, Chantel Williams, Annie Whitman, Anne Wise, Kathy Whitt, MaryAnn Wood, Summer Woody, Mary Ann Yep, and Sue Zabilka, Theresa Zuru, all my ACTS retreat sisters, my Magnificat sisters, my Regnum Christi sisters, my Marian Servant sisters, and so many others whose wing brushed up against my children's wing or my wing during our spiritual journey. Thank you for all the times you loved us, taught us, encouraged us, inspired us, and prayed for us.

I am grateful for my Godparents and my children's Godparents who have assisted us and prayed for us throughout our entire lives. Thank you for your love, prayers, and encouragement.

I am grateful for Deacon Rob who provided spiritual direction during a difficult time in my life. Thank you, Deacon Rob, for telling me that I needed to marry an Italian man, and for praying that a half-Italian man would come into my life. Thank you for providing the Irish blessing at our wedding.

I am grateful for every grandparent, aunt, uncle, cousin, friend, and neighbor who has loved us, rooted for us, or has prayed for my children and me throughout the years.

I am grateful for every saint, angel, priest, deacon, bishop, pope, nun, spiritual director, consecrated woman, consecrated man, teacher, and coach who played a role in my spiritual, educational, and emotional development and that of my family members. Thank you for listening to God's call on your life and for assisting us on our journey.

I am grateful for every doctor and health professional who has brought an increase of health and wellness to me, my husband, my children, step-children, family members, and friends. Thank you for listening to

God's call on your life and for your dedication to the wellbeing of all your patients.

I am grateful for Paul Barbahen. Thank you, Paul, for being a first-class angel of an attorney, for being a friend, and believing in me when I did not believe in myself.

I am grateful for Kary Oberbrunner, my writing coach, for helping me realize that "our greatest source of pain is often our greatest source of impact." Thank you, Kary, for igniting souls, especially mine. Thank you for your much-needed assistance, and most of all for believing that I have what it takes to get my book published and ignite souls.

I am grateful for Erica Foster, who assisted me with much of the publishing and marketing process. Erica without your coaching, I never would have been able to get this book published and out to the public.

I am grateful for Daphne Smith, David Branderhorst, Tanisha Williams, Erica Foster, Abigail Young, Nanette O'Neal and all the staff of Author Academy Elite. Thank you for assisting me with encouraging words or with technical support in front or behind the scenes, during the writing and publishing process.

I am grateful for Pat Gano, Kelly Renee' Baker, and Terry Capshaw. Thank you so much for taking the time out of your busy lives to read my book and for sharing your insights about my book with others. Thank you for your support and your prayers.

I am grateful for the emotional support of the AAE tribe. Thank you for providing your love and support on the Facebook page and when we meet at conferences.

I am grateful for my preview readers: My brother Ray, son John, my daughter Maria, my mom, my brother John, Kelly Gibson, Christine Alwan, Father Pike Thomas, Susan Rothwell, Andrew Tousignant, Anne Wise and everyone else who got a preview of my book and offered feedback. Thank you for your loving encouragement, support, and much-needed feedback during the early, in-between, or late stages of my writing process. Most of all, thank you for believing in me.

I am grateful for Mabel Haselden. Thank you, Mabel, for your calm and peaceful presence during the editing and publishing process. I could never have gotten this book published without your assistance.

I am grateful for Angela Manning. Thank you, Angela, for your encouragement, patience, and assistance with my website and technical support.

I am grateful for Rhonda Lowry. Thank you, Rhonda, for reading my book and offering your insights regarding technicalities and legalities. You greatly reduced my stress during the publishing process.

I am grateful for Radoslaw Krawczyk "Rados" from 99 Designs. Thank you, Radoslaw for sharing your artistic talents with many authors throughout the world and me, and for designing a book cover that was more beautiful than I ever could have imagined. Many thanks to you for your patience during the design and publishing process.

I am grateful for Mother Mary, Saint Joseph, my guardian angel(s), Saint Francis DeSalle, and all the saints in heaven who pray, intercede, or intervene for me, my family, and friends.

I am also grateful for The Poor Clare Sisters, The Carmelites, The Missionaries of Charity, and the communion of saints on Earth who have prayed for me, my family, and friends.

I am grateful for all the first-class angels in my life mentioned, and those who I might have forgotten. The Lord sees your kind deeds and will bless you even more for that which has remained hidden.

Thank you, Lord, for all the amazing people You have brought into my life and the lives of my children who have assisted us on our journey. Dear Lord Jesus, please bless them and their loved ones, cover them with your precious blood, fill them with your Holy Spirit, and carry them in your arms until they arrive safely in heaven. I love You, Lord, Jesus, I praise You and adore You!

About the Author

Francesca Bellamore is a wife, a mother of five children, the stepmother of three children, and a child of God. She can spot a first-class angel just about anywhere, using the eyes of her heart. She has found her niche writing books that contain a repertoire of stories that teach people of all ages how to win at the game of life and love!

Francesca enjoys spending time in prayer, writing, cooking, swimming, and traveling with her husband to visit their eight children, family members, and friends throughout the United States.

She also enjoys public speaking, helping others realize their dreams, party-planning, event-planning, helping other authors get their books published, and taking on missions with other first-class angels.

Connect at:

www.angelmelodies.net

or

francesca@angelmelodies.net

32276874R00173

Made in the USA
Lexington, KY
01 March 2019